Three-Minute Bible Stories with Games, Songs, and Action Plays

by Edith Cutting

illustrated by Becky Radtke

Cover by Dan Grossmann

Copyright © 1994

Shining Star Publications

ISBN No. 0-382-30486-1

Standardized Subject Code TA ac

Printing No. 98765

Shining Star Publications
A Division of Frank Schaffer Publications, Inc.
23740 Hawthorne Boulevard
Torrance, CA 90505-5927

Unless otherwise indicated, the New International Version of the Bible was used in preparing the activities in this book.

DEDICATION

To the Mary Martha Class of the

Sarah Jane Johnson Memorial United Methodist Church

Johnson City, New York

SS3846

TABLE OF CONTENTS

To the Teacher/Parent 4

OLD TESTAMENT STORIES

The Rainbow 5
Jacob's Dream 8
Joseph's Coat 11
Joseph Sees His Brothers Again 14
The Israelites Escape 17
Manna in the Wilderness 20
The Promised Land 23
The Walls of Jericho 26
Ruth and Naomi 29
The Calling of Samuel 32
David and Jonathan 35
Elijah and the Ravens 38
Queen Esther 41
Daniel in the Lions' Den 44
Jonah and the Big Fish 47

NEW TESTAMENT STORIES OF EVENTS

Calming the Storm 50
Jesus in the Temple 53
The Great Catch of Fish 56
Jesus Heals the Paralyzed Man 59
The Centurion's Faith 62
Jesus Heals a Blind Man 65
Zacchaeus 68
Feeding the Five Thousand 71
Washing the Disciples' Feet 74
Feed My Sheep 77

NEW TESTAMENT PARABLES

Parable of the Sower 80
Parable of the Talents 83
Parable of the Good Samaritan 86
Parable of the Lost Sheep 89
Parable of the Lost Son 92
Award Certificate 95
Bookmarks 96

TO THE TEACHER/PARENT

Have you ever been called at 9:30 to substitute-teach a class at 10:00? Do you often wish you had some quick lessons at your fingertips? Many of the songs or choral speakings found in this book will fit in easily and quickly with other church programs or curricula.

The variety of stories from Genesis through the Gospels will help you supplement whatever area your class is studying. The activities are designed to reinforce the stories. The easy-to-sing songs and the games make learning fun and memorable.

The stories are told with short sentences, in an informal style, with explanations of difficult words. These short versions of the stories give quick but coherent reviews or introductions to more complicated Bible stories. Complex stories such as those of Joseph or the prodigal son are reduced to one element of the story, in order to present to children a manageable amount of material.

The stories and activities are adaptable for ages 5-8. The songs are sung to familiar tunes. They may be sung with or without motions. Some of the games may be adapted to different stories with slight variations. For instance, Elijah's relay race (page 40) may be used with the story of Joseph's coat by giving each line of children different colored jackets.

Any way you choose to use the stories and activities in this book, you are sure to find your students listening, singing, playing and learning.

THE RAINBOW
Based on Genesis 8:18-22; 9:8-17

God told Noah to take all the animals on earth, two by two, into the ark to keep them safe from the flood. They were there a long time while the ark floated all around on the water. At last the flood went down, and the ark touched dry land.

After the waters of the flood had gone away, Noah and his family and all the animals and the birds came out of the ark. Noah built an altar to God, and he and his family worshiped God and thanked Him for bringing them safely through the flood.

God was pleased with Noah and happy that all these people and birds and animals were still alive. God promised that He would never again send such a terrible flood to destroy everything on the earth. He said, "As long as the earth endures, seedtime and harvest, cold and heat, summer and winter, day and night will never cease." (*Never cease* means they will never stop. Everything will happen in order just as it always has.) Isn't that a wonderful promise? Let's say it together and act it out.

As long as the earth endures,	*Spread arms wide.*
Seedtime and harvest,	*Raise one arm for each.*
Cold and heat,	*Lower one arm for each.*
Summer and winter,	*Raise one arm for each.*
Day and night	*Lower one arm for each.*
Will never cease.	*Spread arms wide again.*

SS3846

God wanted everybody to know that the world would be safe forever. God wanted people to remember that He would never make such a terrible flood again, so He did something very special.

He told Noah and his sons that He would set a special sign, a rainbow, in the sky. It would be a beautiful, colorful reminder that everyone could see. It would have a stripe of each main color on earth: red, orange, yellow, green, blue, indigo, and violet. Whenever God's rainbow appeared in the sky, it would remind people of the promise He had made. Then God blessed Noah and his sons and put the care of the earth into their hands.

When clouds appear in the sky, sometimes rain falls. We may even see some local flooding of rivers and streams, but never again will God let there be a terrible flood that will destroy everything on earth. The rainbow curving in the sky is the sign of the covenant or agreement between God and all His living things.

RAINBOW COLORS

Draw a rainbow, one color at a time, on the blackboard or a large sheet of paper. As each color is drawn, ask class members to name something that color for which they want to thank God.

COME SEE

Sing these words to the tune "Go Tell Aunt Rhodie" using the appropriate motions.

Come see the rainbow.	*Beckon with both hands.*
Come see the rainbow.	*Beckon with both hands*
Come see the rainbow	*Beckon with both hands.*
God put up in the sky.	*Arch both arms over head.*
It's up above the houses.	*Point up with right hand.*
It's up above the treetops.	*Point up with left hand.*
It's up above the mountains.	*Point up with right hand again.*
It's way up in the sky.	*Arch both arms over head.*
The rainbow is God's promise.	*Clasp hands in prayer position for all*
The rainbow is God's promise.	*three lines.*
The rainbow is God's promise,	
He soon will make things dry.	*Nod head.*
Come see the rainbow.	*Repeat first stanza motions.*
Come see the rainbow.	
Come see the rainbow	
God put up in the sky.	

JACOB'S DREAM

Based on Genesis 28:10-22

Jacob was on his way to the home of his Uncle Laban. It was a long trip and would take him many days. He had camels loaded with food and clothes for the trip, and presents to give the family.

At sunset he stopped for the night. There were no houses anywhere around. Jacob was all by himself. After he took care of his camels, he ate his supper. Then he took a small rock for a pillow and lay down to sleep.

While he was asleep, he had a wonderful dream. Jacob dreamed that there was a stairway reaching from the ground where he lay all the way up to heaven. He dreamed that he saw angels on the stairway going up and down. They were coming and going to do the will of God.

At the top of the stairway in Jacob's dream stood the Lord God Himself. God spoke to Jacob. He promised that He would give Jacob the land where he was sleeping. God also told him that he would have many children and grandchildren to live in that land. Finally God spoke a blessing for all Jacob's people.

When he woke up, Jacob remembered his dream with wonder and awe. He was amazed at all that God had promised. He said, "Surely God is here, and I didn't realize it."

Because God had promised him so much, Jacob wanted to do something special for God. He took the stone that he had used for a pillow and set it up on end. He poured oil on it as if it were an altar and he was making a special offering.

He said, "This place must be the house of God, and the very gate of heaven." He called the place Bethel, which means "the house of God," as a reminder that this was the place where he had dreamed a wonderful dream.

After he poured oil on the altar stone, Jacob made a vow. He promised that if God would protect him on the journey he was taking, the Lord would always be the God of Jacob. Jacob would worship Him and give God His proper share of everything he ever had.

Then Jacob went on his way. He came at last to the home of Laban, his uncle. For many years he worked for Laban, and Jacob married while he was there. But he never forgot seeing the angels going up and down on the stairway from earth to heaven.

JACOB'S DREAM

Sing to the tune of "London Bridge" while using appropriate motions.

Angel feet walked up and down,
Up and down, up and down.
Angel feet walked up and down
In Jacob's dream.

Raise and lower arms while wiggling fingers during first three lines.

Fold hands, close eyes, and rest face sideways on hands.

Above the stairway stood the Lord,
Stood the Lord, stood the Lord.
Above the stairway stood the Lord
In Jacob's dream.

Lift arms and look up during first three lines.

Fold hands, close eyes, and rest face sideways on hands.

Jacob woke and set the stone,
Set the stone, set the stone.
Jacob woke and set the stone
Where he had dreamed.

Bend over, lift, and set the stone during first three lines.

Fold hands, close eyes, and rest face sideways on hands.

"This shall be a sign," he said.
"Sign," he said; "Sign," he said.
"This shall be a sign," he said,
"That God was here!"

Point to stone during first three lines.

Lift arms and face, then point down on last word.

Repeat stanza 1.

JACOB WENT

If you do not have a piano or time to practice a song, try clapping out the rhythm of these simple verses as children chant them. The words may also be sung to the tune of "Jack and Jill" or recited as a jump-rope rhyme.

 Jacob went
Where he was sent,
And found a wife to marry.

On a stone
He slept alone,
But dreamed he saw a stairway.

JOSEPH'S COAT

Based on Genesis 37:3-36

Joseph was younger than most of his brothers. His father, Jacob, loved him especially. Jacob had a beautiful coat of many colors woven for Joseph.

That made Joseph's older brothers jealous. They hated him even more when he told them about two dreams. The dreams seemed to show his family all bowing down to him. His brothers were very angry but didn't do anything about their anger until something else happened.

The older brothers were all away taking care of their father's sheep. One day Jacob decided to send Joseph to see how they were getting along. Joseph was so proud of his coat that he wore it when he went to look for his brothers.

When he got to the place where they should have been, they were not there. A man told him where to find them, so he went on. Before Joseph got to them, his brothers saw him coming. They were so jealous, they decided to kill him and throw his body into a dry cistern there in the field. (A cistern is a deep hole, like a well.)

Joseph's oldest brother, Reuben, objected. "We should not kill him," he said. "Let's just throw him in the dry cistern; then we won't be to blame for shedding his blood."

Reuben meant to get Joseph out of the hole later when his brothers had gone on with their sheep. He intended to take the boy back to their father. But Reuben's sheep were moving, so he had to go take care of them. He didn't see what happened next.

SS3846

When Joseph got to his brothers, they grabbed him, stripped off his beautiful robe, and threw him into the cistern. While they were eating their lunch, some traders rode by on camels. The brothers decided this was their chance to make some money and get rid of Joseph at the same time. They sold Joseph as a slave to the traders, but they kept his beautiful coat.

When Reuben came back, he found that Joseph was gone. He was upset because his plan had not worked. He was the oldest, so he felt responsible. He ran to his brothers and said, "What am I to do?"

The other brothers had begun to think about what they had done. They were worried. What should they tell their father? At last they decided to kill one of their goats and dip Joseph's coat in its blood. They thought their father would blame some wild animal for killing Joseph instead of blaming them.

When Jacob saw Joseph's coat, he recognized it at once. He took it in his hands and said, "Surely some wild beast has killed my son." Then he mourned for Joseph and would not be comforted.

Actually, Joseph was safe in Egypt, working as a slave in an important official's home. But his family didn't know that.

WHERE IS JOSEPH?

This song may be sung in unison or by two groups, one asking the questions and the other answering. Sing it to the tune of "Frere Jacques."

Where is Joseph? Where is Joseph?
In the well. In the well.
Did you take his coat off?
His many-colored coat off?
Here's his coat. Here's his coat.

Where is Joseph? Where is Joseph?
He's not there. He's not there.
He is sold to Egypt,
To be a slave in Egypt.
Here's his coat. Here's his coat.

Where is Joseph? Where is Joseph?
He is gone. He is gone.
We will tell our father
A lion killed our brother.
Here's his coat. Here's his coat.

Where is Joseph? Where is Joseph?
Jacob weeps. Jacob weeps.
We are so ashamed that
We only tell our father,
"Here's his coat. Here's his coat."

JOSEPH FINDS HIS BROTHERS

Have all but two children in the group join hands, standing far apart to represent a flock of sheep. One of the children not in the group should be Joseph; the other one should be a brother. The brother makes himself hard to find by going through the "sheep" toward the center of the circle, then out again, alternating in and out between "sheep" until he returns to his starting place.

"Joseph" must follow in and out the same way, trying to catch his brother. When he does tag him, the brother becomes Joseph, and a new brother is chosen. If he is unsuccessful, both Joseph and his brother become sheep, and new contestants try.

JOSEPH SEES HIS BROTHERS AGAIN

Based on Genesis 41–45

Years after Joseph was sold into slavery by his brothers, he became a ruler of Egypt. His brothers did not know that. They thought he was lost forever.

During that time, there was a terrible famine in Israel. (A famine means that there was no food. The earth was so dry, no grain could grow, so people could not make bread.) There was a famine in Egypt, too, but Joseph had stored lots of grain from other years. Many people came to Egypt to buy grain.

Among the men who came were Joseph's older brothers. They did not recognize him. He was grown up, of course, and dressed like a rich man. Joseph recognized his brothers but he did not tell them who he was. He only asked about the family. He wanted to know about his father and his younger brother, Benjamin.

Joseph decided to test his brothers. Would they treat Benjamin as they had once treated him? He told them they could have grain this time because he didn't want anybody to starve, but if they ever wanted more, they must bring their youngest brother with them.

The brothers didn't want to do that, and they knew their father, Jacob, would not want them to either. Weeks went by, and the grain they had bought in Egypt was used up. They had to get more, and the only place with extra grain was Egypt!

At last Jacob agreed that Benjamin could go to Egypt with the others. When they got there, Joseph still did not tell them who he was.

He let them have grain, but he hid his own silver cup in Benjamin's sack of grain. Then he pretended it had been stolen. When the cup was found in Benjamin's sack, Joseph said that Benjamin must stay in Egypt and be his slave.

The brothers said they would all be Joseph's slaves. One of the older brothers begged that Benjamin be sent home. He said he would be Joseph's slave in place of Benjamin. He explained that he could not bear to see his father's face if Benjamin did not come home.

At last Joseph was sure his brothers did not want to hurt their father or brother. He told them that he was Joseph, the brother they had thought was lost. He told them to go home, get their father, and come back to live in Egypt with him.

They were all so glad, they kissed one another and cried and shouted. All Jacob's sons were together again, and their father would soon be with them too.

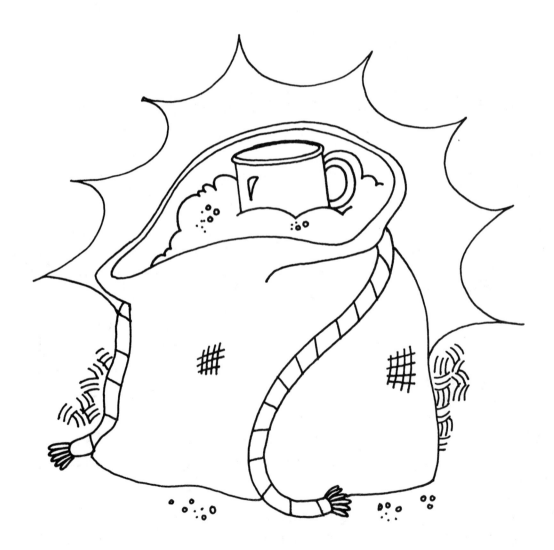

SS3846

JOSEPH'S CUP

Form a tight circle with all but one child facing the center. Have one child stand in the center of the circle to represent Joseph. The circle members stand close together but do not hold hands. They pass a silver cup (plastic cup covered with foil) behind them, trying to keep Joseph from seeing who has it. The passing motions should be going on continuously.

When Joseph points at someone and says, "Benjamin," everyone must hold still, all passing stopped. The one pointed at holds up his hands. If he has the cup, he becomes "Joseph." If not, the game continues until someone is caught with the cup.

JOSEPH'S BROTHERS IN EGYPT

Young children will enjoy "marching to Egypt" rhythm as they say this rhyme. Start with the left foot, stamping on the strong first beat.

Joseph, Joseph,
Have you any food?
Yes, sir, yes, sir,
Grain that's good.

Food for my people
And those everywhere.
Our God gave us plenty
So that now we can share.

These words may also be sung to the tune of "Baa, Baa, Black Sheep."

THE ISRAELITES ESCAPE
Based on Exodus 12:31-32; 14:5-31

Long after Joseph and his family lived in Egypt, a new Pharaoh, the king of Egypt, made all Israelites work as slaves. They were slaves for years and years; then God wanted them to be free. He told Moses to ask Pharaoh to let the Israelites go.

Moses asked Pharaoh to let the Israelites leave, but Pharaoh said, "No!" God sent plagues to disturb the Egyptians and convince Pharaoh to free the Israelites, but the answer was still, "No!"

At last, God told Moses to be ready to leave on a certain night. On that night God promised that Pharaoh would change his mind. God was going to make the Egyptians so fearful and unhappy, they would all want the Israelites to leave.

That's just what happened. Pharaoh called Moses to him that night and told him to take his people out of Egypt at once with all their sheep and cows. Moses rushed back to the Israelites and told them they were leaving.

They hurried away that very night. But it was a long trip. Day after day passed, and they began to feel tired and discouraged.

Back in Egypt, Pharaoh and his officials changed their minds. "Now we don't have slaves any more," they said. "We don't have anyone to do our work. Let's go after the Israelites and bring them back."

Pharaoh called for his best chariots, hundreds of them. They were fast, two-wheeled wagons with horses and drivers. They all set out to chase the Israelites.

Shining Star Publications, Copyright © 1994 SS3846

When the Israelites saw the Egyptians coming, they were afraid. They were camped near the edge of the Red Sea and could not go ahead because of all the water! They could not go back because the Egyptians were coming.

Then God said to Moses, "Raise your staff and stretch out your arm towards the sea. I will send a great wind to blow the waters back, so My people can go through on dry land."

Moses raised his arm, and a great wind divided the sea. All the Israelites with all their sheep and cows walked safely through the sea.

The Egyptians tried to drive their chariots through the divided sea, but their wheels got stuck, and the chariots broke down.

When all the Israelites had safely reached the other side, God said to Moses, "Stretch out your hand again." Moses did, and the water all flowed back and covered the Egyptians. Not one of them escaped.

The Israelites were safe on the other side. They praised God and trusted His servant, Moses, to lead them where they should go.

THE RED SEA

Divide the class into three groups. One group should join hands in a circle to be the Red Sea; one group should form a line of Israelites with Moses leading them; the third group should be Egyptians. (If the class is small, one pupil may represent the Israelites and one the Egyptians. This will leave the rest of the class to represent the Red Sea and surround the Egyptians.)

During the first two stanzas, the Israelites march around the room and up to the Red Sea. When Moses reaches out his arm, the Red Sea circle divides into two parallel lines to let the Israelites through. When the Egyptians approach, the lines re-form the circle, surrounding them.

Sing to the tune of "Itsy Bitsy Spider."

The Israelites left Egypt's land.	The Red Sea opened wide and dry
They wanted to be free.	To let God's people through:
Great Moses led them	Men, women, children,
Onward to the sea.	Sheep, and cattle too.
There God was with them	Then came Egyptians
And kept them safe from harm,	With horses wild and fast,
For Moses did what God had said,	But the Red Sea closed its waves again
And he stretched out his arm.	And would not let them past.

LEAVING EGYPT

The Israelites had to go slowly as they left Egypt because they were taking their sheep and cows with them. Choose a child to be Moses. He is the shepherd. All the rest of the children bend or squat and grasp their ankles with their hands, thus representing sheep. Moses leads the sheep as they try to reach the Red Sea (the opposite side of the room). The first sheep who reaches the other side of the room without losing hold of his ankles becomes the new Moses. All others return to the starting line and a new race begins. This time they may grasp their knees (because cows are taller than sheep) as they try to reach the Red Sea.

MANNA IN THE WILDERNESS
Based on Exodus 16:14-35

After the Israelites had crossed the Red Sea, they wandered in the desert for a long time. They ate all the bread and used the flour they had brought with them. They got tired of the food they had and forgot that they had promised to trust God. Every day they complained to Moses. At last Moses took his problem to God. He asked what to do about the people's complaining.

God said to Moses, "I will send down food as if it were raining! Have each person pick up enough to eat for just one day. The next morning more food will rain down. On the sixth day everyone is to pick up enough for two days. They are not to work on the Sabbath, so no food will come down on that day. Let them hear and obey."

The next morning when people looked out of their tents, they saw a heavy dew on the ground. After that dried up, there was a thin layer of little things that looked like snowflakes on the ground.

"What is that?" people asked. They had never seen anything like it before.

"That is the food the Lord has sent," Moses told them. It looked like small, white seeds. When they put some in their mouths, it was sweet, like honey-flavored crackers. They called it manna.

Moses told the people what God had said. They were to pick up all they would need for one day, but not keep any overnight. When they had picked up all they needed, the rest melted away.

20

SS3846

Some people listened and did as Moses said, but some did not. Some people picked up too much that first day. They thought they would have enough left over so that they would not have to pick up any the next day. When they got up the next morning, they found that the leftover manna had spoiled. It smelled terrible, and there were maggots, ugly little worms, crawling in it.

Then came the sixth day, and most people picked up twice as much. Moses said that was right because the next day was the Sabbath. They were not to work on the Sabbath, so of course they should not pick up manna then.

Again, some people didn't pay attention. In spite of what Moses had told them, they did not gather extra for the Sabbath. They went out for manna the morning of the Sabbath, but there was nothing there. Those people had to go hungry that day.

At last the Israelites learned to do as God told them. For forty years God sent them manna. They boiled or baked it or fixed it any way they liked. They ate it every day until they arrived in the land God had promised them.

TASTING MANNA

Have the children put their heads down, eyes closed, to simulate night. While they are not looking, spread a sheet on the floor and cover it with Cheerios™ or other children's cereal. (Oatmeal would probably look more like manna, but children would be discouraged to try to pick up a cupful! Besides, it would not have the sweet taste.)

Wake the class for "morning" and give each a small paper cup to be filled with the day's ration. (They may eat what they want after each has filled a cup, but not while they are picking up the manna.)

HAVE YOU HEARD?

This song may be sung to the tune of "Did You Ever See a Lassie?" You may want to let children pretend to gather manna as they sing.

Have you heard about the manna,
The manna, the manna?
Have you heard about the manna
In God's wilderness?

He sent it to the hungry,
Like dewdrops of sweetness.
Have you heard about the manna
In God's wilderness?

Let us gather up the manna,
The manna, the manna.
Let us gather up the manna
God gives us today.

We'll eat it and thank Him
For sending it to us.
Let us gather up the manna
God gives us today.

THE PROMISED LAND

Based on Numbers 13:1-2, 17-33; 14:1-3, 26-30

The Israelites had come near to the land God had promised them. The Lord told Moses to send some men ahead to explore the country. Moses appointed twelve men, one from each tribe, to go see what the Promised Land was like.

He told them to find out if there were many people and if they were big or little. He told them to find out if the cities had high walls around them. "Find out if the ground is good," he said. He even told them to bring back some of the fruit of the land if they could.

The twelve men went into the land. They looked at the land and cities and the people. After forty days they came back to share what they had seen. They even brought back a bunch of grapes so big that two men had to carry it on a pole between them. (Bring a bunch of grapes to class to show how much bigger those were in the Promised Land.)

The men all said it was a rich land, "flowing with milk and honey." ("Flowing with milk and honey" were the words people used in those days to mean that there were lots of good things to eat and drink there.)

But ten of the men were afraid of this new land. They said there were big cities with high walls around them and the people were giants! "The men were so big," they said, "that we seemed like little grasshoppers!"

Two of the men did not agree with the others. Caleb and Joshua were not afraid. They said, "Let's do what the Lord wants us to. The Lord is with us. We can do what He tells us to." Even though there were big walled cities, Caleb and Joshua were sure God would help them.

Still, the other ten men were so afraid that they frightened the people listening to them. They worried about the giants. They wanted to go back to Egypt to get away from them. They cried and grumbled and had an awful time.

When God heard them, He was very angry. He said if the people didn't want to go to the rich and beautiful land He had promised them, then He would never let them go there. Instead, they would have to live in the desert wilderness for the rest of their lives.

Only Caleb and Joshua wanted to go where God had told them to go. Those two men would get to live in the Promised Land. None of the other grown-ups ever would. But Joshua would lead the children who grew up in the wilderness. Caleb also would go with him into the land "flowing with milk and honey," the Promised Land.

I SPY

"I Spy" is a game that may be used to remind children of the purpose of the twelve people sent to explore the Promised Land. Before class, hide around the room a variety of goods that might have been found in the Promised Land: grapes, figs, other fruits and vegetables, packages of seeds, stalks of grain, a jar of honey, a small carton of milk, etc. The fruits and vegetables may be real or plastic, but if possible, have a large bunch of seedless grapes for the children to eat after all the produce has been found and brought back from the "Promised Land."

THE PROMISED LAND

Have the class sing this song with the appropriate motions. Sing it to the tune of the first part of "Oh, Dear, What Can the Matter Be?"

Come, come, come to the Promised Land.　　*Beckon with both hands first three*
Come, come, come to the Promised Land.　　　*lines.*
Come, come, come to the Promised Land
Where milk and honey are found.　　　　　　*Open arms wide.*

We're afraid of the people there;　　　　　　*Jerk hands in rejecting motion, in*
We're afraid of the giants there;　　　　　　　*time with music, during first three*
We're afraid of the cities there;　　　　　　　*lines.*
They have high walls all around.　　　　　　　*Join hands in closed circle above head.*

Stay, stay, stay in the desert then.　　　　　　*Use bigger rejection motions.*
Stay, stay, stay in the desert then.
Stay, stay, stay in the desert then.
Only your children shall go.　　　　　　　　　*Put hands down to indicate short people.*

Led by Caleb and Joshua,　　　　　　　　　　*Hold up one finger on each hand and*
Led by Caleb and Joshua,　　　　　　　　　　*shake to stress.*
Into, into the Promised Land　　　　　　　　　*Stretch out arms in generous,*
All of your children shall go.　　　　　　　　　*inclusive gesture.*

This song may be turned into a singing skit by having one group of children sing the first, third, and fourth stanzas, and another group sing the second.

THE WALLS OF JERICHO

Based on Joshua 6:1-20

The time had finally come for the Israelites to go into the Promised Land. Many of them had been afraid of the giants and the walled cities there. Joshua and Caleb had said that with God's help they could conquer the land. Now all who had not wanted to go into the new land had died, so God let the others enter the Promised Land. Moses, too, had died. Joshua was now the leader.

He led them safely across the Jordan River. Ahead of them was the great city of Jericho. It had high walls all around it. The Israelites thought it looked as if nobody could go in or out. How could they fight and conquer such a mighty city?

Before they even had time to worry about it, a messenger came to Joshua from the Lord. This was the message he brought: Joshua was to have all the Israelites march around the city once each day for six days. Seven priests with trumpets of rams' horns and men carrying the ark of the covenant were to march ahead of them. (The covenant was the agreement God and the Israelites had made with one another. The ark was a special chest that held important items to remind the people of God's care.)

The Israelites following the ark of the covenant showed that they were following God's plan. God's promise was leading them. Each day for six days they were to march around the city of Jericho without saying a word. The trumpets were to be the only sound. Then everybody was to go back into camp.

On the seventh day, the people were to march around the city seven times, keeping quiet until the end of the seventh time around. Then Joshua would command, "Shout!" At his command, everybody was to shout as loud as he could and run at the walls. God promised that the walls would fall down. Everybody could get in, and the city would be conquered.

The Israelites did what the Lord had commanded them. Quietly each day for six days they walked once around the city of Jericho. On the seventh day, they walked quietly around Jericho seven times. Then Joshua commanded, "Shout, for the Lord has given you the city!" The people all shouted at the top of their lungs and ran right into the city. The walls fell down before them. They had conquered the great city of Jericho by doing exactly as the Lord had told them.

SS3846

JERICHO FALLS DOWN

Arrange a dozen or more large cardboard cartons in the center of the floor to represent the city of Jericho. Let one child represent a priest, carrying a horn of some kind (or with his hand circling his mouth to represent a trumpet). Let another child carry a jewel box or something comparable to represent the ark of the covenant. Have the class walk silently around the city six times, returning to their seats after each time, to mark the six days.

The seventh time they should keep going around seven times. When Joshua (the teacher) says, "Shout!" all the children shout and run forward, pushing the cartons down.

A SIMPLER CONQUEST

If you have a smaller space or need a less boisterous activity, this motion play may be used. Place hands together, the palm of one on the back of the other. At the count (1st day, 2nd day, etc.) lift the top hand and bring it around the other, returning it to its original position. On the seventh day, do seven such circles; then shout and throw up your arms in rejoicing.

CRASH! BANG!

Use the hand motions while singing this song to the tune of "She'll Be Comin' Round the Mountain."

We'll go once around the city
  for six days. (Sh! Sh!)
We'll go once around the city
  for six days. (Sh! Sh!)
We'll go once around the city.
We'll go once around the city.
We'll go once around the city
  for six days. (Sh! Sh!)

Hold up one finger, then six fingers, then put one to the lips. Repeat for second and fifth lines.

Hold up one finger.
Hold up one finger.
Repeat second line motions.

On the seventh we'll go 'round it
  seven times. (Sh! Sh!)
On the seventh we'll go 'round it
  seven times. (Sh! Sh!)
On the seventh we'll go 'round it.
On the seventh we'll go 'round it.
On the seventh we'll go 'round it
  seven times. (Crash! Bang!)

Hold up seven fingers, then one to lips. Repeat for second line.

Hold up seven fingers quietly; lower them at end of line; then raise again.

Shout and clap loudly.

RUTH AND NAOMI

Based on Ruth 1–2:12; 4:13, 17

It was a time of famine in Israel. (*Famine* means there were no crops or food.) Many people went to other countries to work and buy food. Naomi went with her husband and two sons into the land of Moab. They made a home there and stayed for many years. Naomi's two sons married Moabite girls, Orpah and Ruth.

Life was hard in Moab. Naomi's husband died; then her two sons died. The famine was no longer causing people to starve in Israel. Naomi decided that the best thing for her to do, now that she had no husband and no sons, was to go back to Israel where she had other relatives.

When she started back, Ruth and Orpah walked part of the way with her. They both loved her and were afraid they might never see her again. After they had walked some way, Naomi told her daughters-in-law that they should turn back and stay in their own land. Orpah agreed. She kissed Naomi good-bye and turned back.

But Ruth would not go back. She said she would always stay with Naomi, her mother-in-law, whom she loved. "Don't urge me to leave you," she said. "Where you go, I will go, and where you stay, I will stay. Your people will be my people, and your God my God." She even told Naomi, "Where you die, I will die, and there will I be buried." After Ruth had said this, she called on God to hear her promise that she would stay with Naomi all the rest of her life.

SS3846

When Naomi saw Ruth was determined, they went on together until they came to Naomi's home in Bethlehem. They lived there together, with Naomi keeping the house and Ruth going into the fields to glean. (*Glean* means that she picked up stalks of grain that the men who harvested the field had left.) By gleaning, she and Naomi had grain to make bread.

One day while Ruth was gleaning, the owner of the field came by. His name was Boaz. When he saw Ruth and heard how good she was to her mother-in-law, he decided to be good to her. He told his men to leave extra grain for her.

After a time, Boaz and Ruth were married. They had a baby whom they named Obed. Years later, Obed had a grandson named David, who became king of Israel. King David was an ancestor of Jesus. (Ancestors are people in your family who lived before you were born.)

We remember these two women because Ruth loved Naomi so much that she went to Israel to live with her and worship God. God blessed Ruth by making her one of the ancestors of Jesus. Ruth and Boaz lived happily together and took care of Naomi as long as she lived.

RUTH'S PROMISE

Let one child be Ruth while all the rest act as a chorus, saying the introductory words of her promise. This may be done several times with different girls taking the part of Ruth.

Chorus	**Ruth**
Don't urge me to leave you	Or to turn back from you.
Where you go,	I will go.
And where you stay,	I will stay.
Your people will be my people	And your God, my God.
Where you die,	I will die, and there will I be buried!

Teacher: And that's the promise that Ruth kept all her life!

A GLEANING GAME

Scatter several dozen paper or plastic straws on the floor to represent grain left by reapers.

Choose a child to be Naomi, sitting on the floor at one side of the room where she is at home. Everybody else gleans, picking up as many straws as possible with one hand. When all the straws have been picked up, each child brings his handful to Naomi. Help Naomi count each child's straws. The one who has the most is named Ruth. Naomi may then reward each one with a cracker such as might have been made from the grain.

THE CALLING OF SAMUEL
Based on 1 Samuel 1:10-11, 20; 3:2-10, 19-20

Samuel was a little boy in Israel. His mother's name was Hannah, and his father's name was Elkanah. They had wanted a little boy so badly that Hannah had prayed to God, asking Him to give her a son. She promised that if she could have a son, she would give him to the Lord. She would send him to the temple to be a helper.

After Hannah prayed so hard, God gave her a baby. She named him Samuel. Day after day Hannah took care of her baby, but she did not forget her promise to God. When Samuel was big enough to take care of himself, Hannah took him to the temple. She told Eli, the priest, that she had promised to give her son to the Lord. The little boy was to live at the temple, learning all that Eli could teach him. He was to serve God in every way he could. So Samuel grew up in the temple. He did all he could to help Eli, and Eli was like a father to him.

One night after Samuel had gone to bed, a voice called to him. Samuel answered, "Here I am." Then he ran to Eli because he thought it was Eli who had called him.

Eli said, "I did not call you. Go back and lie down."

Samuel went back to bed. He had hardly gone to sleep when the voice called again. "Samuel!" it said.

"Here I am," Samuel answered. He ran to Eli again.

SS3846

Eli said, "My son, I did not call. Go back and lie down."

Again Samuel went back to bed. He knew somebody had called him. Who could it have been? He was puzzled, but he lay down and went to sleep. A little later he was awakened again by someone calling, "Samuel."

Once more he ran to Eli. "Here I am," he said. "You called me."

Then Eli realized that it was God who was calling Samuel. "Go back to bed," he said to the boy, "and if God calls you again say, 'Speak, Lord. I am your servant, and I am listening.'"

Samuel went back to bed. He lay there quietly, wondering what was going to happen. Soon he heard the voice again. This time it was near, as if someone were standing by his bed. "Samuel," the Lord said. "Samuel."

Samuel answered as Eli had told him. "Speak, my Lord," he said. "I am your servant, and I am listening to you."

Then the Lord gave him a message. He knew Samuel was ready to do God's will because every time He had called Samuel had answered, "Here I am." From that night on, people all over Israel knew that Samuel was a messenger of God.

HERE I AM

This choral speaking may be done several times with different members of the group taking the solo part.

Solo: Here I am.   *Raise arms toward heaven.*
                Here I am.   *Bring hands back to chest.*

Chorus: That was Samuel's answer.

Solo: Here I am.   *Raise arms, then bring them back to chest.*

Chorus: Here we are.   *All raise arms toward heaven.*
                Here we are.   *Bring hands back to chest.*

Solo: That shall be our answer, Lord,   *Raise arms again.*
                Whenever You shall call.

Chorus: Here we are, Lord!   *All raise arms toward heaven and*
                Here we are!   *hold them up.*

THE CALLING OF SAMUEL

The leader holds up a small stone (or toy or ball small enough to be concealed in a child's hand). One child is designated as Samuel and leaves the room. The other children form a circle, sitting on the floor and holding out their hands. The leader goes all around the circle, touching each pair of hands, leaving the stone in one. Everybody closes his hands as the leader passes so no one else knows who has the stone.

The leader then calls, "Samuel." The missing child comes back in. He looks at the children's closed hands and faces. They pretend guilt or innocence to keep "Samuel" from knowing who has the stone. He has three guesses. If one is right, the person holding the stone becomes Samuel for the continuing game. If none of Samuel's guesses is right, he must go out and try again (or he may be allowed to choose someone to be the next Samuel).

SS3846

DAVID AND JONATHAN
Based on 1 Samuel 18:1-9; 20:1-42

After David killed the giant Goliath, the Israelites were grateful and very proud of him. King Saul honored him even though David was only a shepherd boy. Saul gave him a place in his own household. He made him an officer in the army. Often Saul had David play on the harp because the king liked to listen to music.

Saul's son, Jonathan, and David became very good friends. Jonathan gave David his own beautiful robe, a sword, and a bow with arrows. David and Jonathan made a covenant (a promise or agreement) that they would be best friends forever.

At first, everything went well. David did whatever King Saul asked of him. In fact, the trouble began because David did everything so well. He became so popular that a song was written about him. When he came back from battle, women danced in the streets and sang, "Saul has slain his thousands, and David his tens of thousands."

That made King Saul jealous. It sounded as if David was a greater fighter than the king! From then on, Saul hated him and made up his mind to kill David.

David realized that the king was his enemy, but Jonathan didn't think so. He could not believe that his own father would be an enemy of his best friend. Jonathan made a plan to find out for sure how his father felt about David.

According to the plan, David would not come to supper for two nights. Instead, he would hide by a big rock in a field. During that time Jonathan would talk with his father. He would find out how Saul felt about David. Then Jonathan would go to the field where David was hiding and shoot arrows near the rock. He would bring a servant with him to collect the arrows.

This was the secret code Jonathan planned. He might shout to his servant, "The arrows are on this side of you. Bring them here." That would mean that David could come to him. Saul was not angry. But if Jonathan shouted, "The arrows are beyond you," David must go away from him to be safe.

Jonathan talked with his father and found out that Saul was very jealous of David. He even said that David must die! Jonathan was so upset he couldn't even eat his supper.

In the morning Jonathan went to the field and shot arrows. He shouted to his servant, "Isn't the arrow beyond you? Hurry! Go quickly." This was Jonathan's way of warning David of what danger he was in.

He sent the servant home with his bow and arrows. After the servant had gone, Jonathan ran to the place where David was hiding. David and Jonathan said good-bye.

Before David left, Jonathan reminded him of their covenant. No matter how Saul felt, they had promised to be friends forever. That is why, when we speak of good friends today, we remember David and Jonathan.

THEY WERE FRIENDS

Sing this song to the tune of "The Bear Came Over the Mountain."

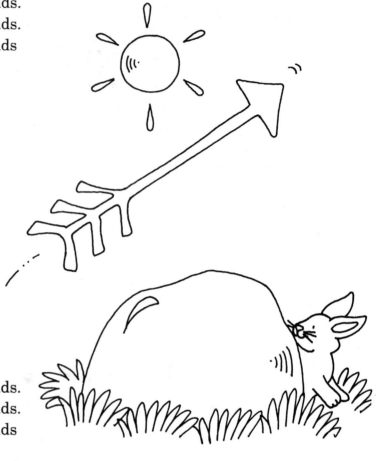

David and Jonathan, they were friends.
David and Jonathan, they were friends.
David and Jonathan, they were friends
A long, long time ago.

Jonathan's father was David's foe.
Jonathan's father was David's foe.
Jonathan's father was David's foe
A long, long time ago.

David was hiding away from Saul.
David was hiding away from Saul.
David was hiding away from Saul
When Jonathan drew his bow.

He shot an arrow beyond the rock.
He shot an arrow beyond the rock.
He shot an arrow beyond the rock
To tell his friend to go.

David and Jonathan, they were friends.
David and Jonathan, they were friends.
David and Jonathan, they were friends
Wherever they might go.

DAVID AND JONATHAN

Each two players form a David-and-Jonathan team, one standing behind the other, holding him firmly by the shoulders. One or two single players left are Saul(s). Saul tries to attach himself to a team by putting his hands on the shoulder of any second team member. The pairs twist and turn to try to keep him from doing so. When he does succeed, the front one of the pair must drop off and become Saul. He then tries to attach himself to some other pair. The game continues as different Davids have to drop off and become Saul.

ELIJAH AND THE RAVENS

Based on 1 Kings 16:30-33; 17:1-6

Elijah was a great prophet of the Lord who did many wonderful things. One of the things he is most remembered for is not what he did, but what God did for him. God protected him when wicked King Ahab wanted to kill him.

Ahab was king of Israel. He did more bad things than any of the kings before him. He married an evil woman named Jezebel who had many of the Lord's prophets killed. Ahab made an idol to Jezebel's false god, Baal, and worshiped the idol instead of the Lord.

Elijah scolded Ahab for his sins and tried to get Ahab to change his wicked ways. Ahab would not listen. He just got worse and worse.

Finally Elijah warned Ahab of punishment to come. There was going to be a terrible drought in Israel. Elijah said, "There will be neither dew nor rain in the next few years unless I call for it in the name of the Lord, the God of Israel." That meant there would be no water for anybody in the country as long as Ahab continued his wickedness.

The Lord knew Ahab would be angry with Elijah. Ahab would probably try to kill him. So God told Elijah to leave the place where he was, where Ahab's men could find him, and go east to hide in the Kerith Valley, east of the Jordan River. That would be outside Ahab's kingdom. Elijah could drink from Kerith Brook. He would have water while all the rivers in Ahab's kingdom were drying up.

Elijah did as the Lord told him and escaped from Ahab. He still did not know how he was to get food. He had to stay hidden in the Kerith Valley, but he trusted God to take care of him.

God knew Elijah's needs, and He was so great He could command everything in nature. He told the ravens that lived near Kerith Brook to help Elijah. (Ravens are big black birds, bigger than crows.)

They were to bring bread and meat every morning to the bank of the Kerith Brook where Elijah would be waiting for them. In the evening, they were to bring more bread and meat to the same place.

For many days Elijah drank water from the Kerith Brook and ate food that the Lord sent to him by the ravens. He was safe from Ahab in Kerith Valley and he had water and food, while Ahab's country was drying up. God took good care of Elijah.

SS3846

FEEDING ELIJAH RELAY RACE

Divide the class into two groups, one to carry meat and one to carry bread to Elijah. Give each child in one group a representation of bread (a card with the word on it or a picture of bread, etc.) and each child in the other line a similar representation of meat. Give each leader a small basket. Have Elijah sit in the front of the room and the two teams line up at the back.

At the starting signal the leader in each row puts his bread or meat into the basket and "flies" to Elijah, holding his basket with arms waving. He empties the basket by Elijah and flies back to give the next person in line the basket. Whichever line gets all its bread or meat to Elijah first wins.

GO, ELIJAH, GO

Sing this song to the tune of "Old MacDonald Had a Farm."

Old Elijah ran away — Go, Elijah, go —
When unto him the Lord did say, "Go, Elijah, go.
Find the Kerith Valley
With its cool, cool brook,
Where Ahab will not think to look.
There I'll keep you safe indeed.
Elijah, you'll have all you need."

Old Elijah ran away — Go, Elijah, go —
When unto him the Lord did say, "Go, Elijah, go."
He found Kerith Brook
With its water sweet,
And ravens brought him bread and meat.
He had good water, and he was fed.
Elijah did what God had said.

QUEEN ESTHER
Based on Esther 2:5–4:16; 8:3-11

Esther was a beautiful Jewish girl who lived in Persia long, long ago. After her mother and father died, she was adopted and brought up by her cousin, Mordecai. Esther was a kind girl, and everybody liked her.

The king of Persia was looking for a new queen. Many pretty girls were brought for him to choose from. When he saw Esther, he chose her and set the royal crown on her head. She became Queen Esther.

There was much celebration in the country of Persia. The king had a great banquet and gave gifts to many people. He did not know or care that Esther was Jewish. She was beautiful and kind, and he admired her.

Some time after Esther became queen, two men plotted to kill the king. Esther's cousin, Mordecai, found out about the plot and sent word to her. She told the king, and his life was saved. He was very grateful to Mordecai.

One man in the king's court was very jealous of Esther's cousin. Haman, the king's adviser, knew that Mordecai was Jewish, so he planned to have all the Jewish people in the whole kingdom killed. Haman thought he would get rid of Mordecai that way. When Mordecai heard of this terrible plan, he sent word to Esther. He asked her to talk to the king to save her people.

Queen Esther didn't know what to do. She was not supposed to go before the king unless he called for her. He could even order her to be killed if she disobeyed that rule. She sent word to Mordecai about how dangerous it would be for her to try to talk to the king.

Mordecai sent a stern message back to her: "You must save your people. Who knows? Maybe God made you queen for this very reason, to save your people."

Esther was worried. She wanted to save her family and friends, but what if the king ordered her to be killed? She made up her mind that whatever happened, she must talk to the king. She must ask him not to do this terrible thing that Haman had planned.

She sent her answer to Mordecai. Queen Esther told him to have all the Jewish people get together and fast for three days (that meant they would not eat or drink for three days) while they prayed to God to take care of her and help her people. She and all her maids in the palace would fast and pray too. Then she would go to the king.

She finished her message with the brave words, "If I perish, I perish." (*Perish* means to die.) She meant that she would do the best she could. If she was killed, at least she would have tried to save her people.

Queen Esther did not perish. She was able to convince the king. He issued an order that gave the Jewish people the right to defend themselves. From that day to this, Queen Esther has been honored for risking her life to save her people.

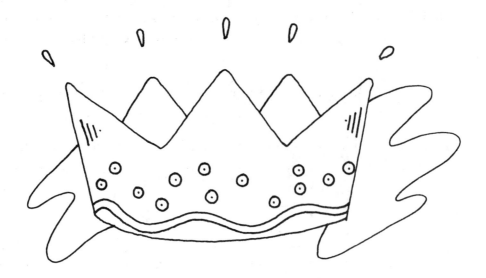

QUEEN ESTHER'S CROWN

Make a tagboard or construction paper crown with gold cord and sequin decorations on the front. On the floor, mark two circles in chalk at a distance from each other.

Players take turns standing in a circle and trying to throw the crown at the other circle. If it touches the circle, give two points. If it lands inside the circle, give five points. The tossing may be repeated until one person has a score of ten or twenty, or until time runs out. The highest scorer gets to wear the crown home.

SAVED BY QUEEN ESTHER

Sing this song with appropriate motions to the tune of "Good King Wenceslas."

Haman planned to kill all Jews
In every Persian city.
No one else dared tell the king
Or ask him to take pity.

Spread both hands out, palms and
  thumbs down.
Shake head.
Clasp hands and bow.

Good Queen Esther, she was brave;
Her people she did cherish.
She would ask the king herself,
Even if she perished.

Hand on heart.
Hugging motion.
Lift right hand as if taking an oath.
Shrug.

To the great hall Esther went,
And asked the king to save them.
He loved Esther and agreed;
The right to live he gave them.

Clasp hands and bow.

Nod head.
Extend hands, palms up.

Good Queen Esther, she was brave;
Her people she did cherish.
Because she dared to do God's will
He did not let her perish!

Hand on heart.
Hugging motion.
Lift right hand.
Smile and shake head.

DANIEL IN THE LIONS' DEN

Based on Daniel 6:3-26

Daniel was an Israelite who had been captured by the Persians. They treated him well, and he became a high official in their country. Still, he worshiped God. He knelt and prayed to God three times every day.

Other officials were jealous and wanted to get rid of Daniel. They went to the Persian king and said, "We ask you to make a new law so that when a person prays to anybody but you, he will be thrown into the lions' den."

The king was proud, and without thinking, he agreed to the law.

When Daniel learned about the law, he went home and prayed to God just as he had always done. The other officials went to Daniel's home, too, and spied on him.

Then they went to the king and said, "Didn't you make a law that whoever prayed to anybody but you should be thrown into the lions' den?" The king said he had. Then the officials told him that Daniel was praying to his God three times a day just as he had always done.

King Darius was very upset. He liked Daniel and did not want to have him thrown into the lions' den. But the other officials reminded him that the law could not be changed, even by the king.

SS3846

That night King Darius ordered Daniel to be thrown into the lions' den. He was so sorry to do it that he said to Daniel, "May your God rescue you!" The lions' den was closed with a big rock. The king himself sealed it with the print of his special ring. King Darius went home, but he could not sleep. He was too worried. The next morning he rushed to the lions' den and called to Daniel to ask if God had saved him.

Daniel answered, "Oh, yes, great king. My God sent his angel to shut the mouths of the lions, and they have not hurt me!"

The king gave orders to have Daniel lifted out at once. He was perfectly safe. Then he ordered the men who had accused Daniel to be thrown into the lions' den themselves.

King Darius issued a new law. He said that God had been great enough to keep Daniel safe even in the lions' den. Therefore, everybody in Persia should fear and worship the God of Daniel.

SS3846

THE STORY OF DANIEL

Ask children to make the following sounds and motions as the story is read.

1. Every time the lions' den is mentioned, growl (grr) and hold up both hands with fingers curved like claws.

2. When Daniel says that an angel shut the mouths of the lions, curve your claw-like fingers down to the thumb and keep quiet.

3. Every time God or prayer is mentioned, fold both hands in prayer position and bow your head.

IN THE LIONS' DEN

One child represents Daniel. All the others are lions. The lions stand in a circle around Daniel, holding hands. Daniel tries to get out of the circle, but the lions try to keep him in by closing any gap where he tries to escape. He must quickly try one after another. The lions must keep holding hands and may not take hold of Daniel or strike him. (Remember, God did not let the lions hurt Daniel.) When he escapes, he chooses the next person to be Daniel.

SS3846

JONAH AND THE BIG FISH

Based on Jonah 1–3

Jonah believed in God, but he did not want to do what God told him to do. Instead, he tried to run away.

God had told Jonah to go to Nineveh. That was a great city, but a very wicked one. God wanted the people there to repent and be good, so He sent Jonah to warn them. Instead of going to Nineveh though, Jonah got on a ship for Tarshish in the opposite direction!

After the ship set sail, Jonah went to sleep. He didn't realize when a terrible storm hit. The wind made tremendous waves. The sailors threw cargo overboard to lighten the ship, and each one prayed to his god. Nothing helped. The storm grew worse.

The captain found Jonah asleep. He told Jonah to wake up and pray to his God as the others were doing.

At the same time, the sailors drew lots to see who was to blame for the dreadful storm. They found out it was Jonah. They asked him who his God was, and why his God was punishing him.

Jonah told them he worshiped the Lord God who had made all the land and the sea. Jonah told the sailors he was trying to run away from God. He even told them to throw him into the sea, and it would become calm.

The sailors didn't want to throw anybody into the sea to drown. They tried to row back to land, but the storm got worse and worse. At last they did what Jonah had told them to do. They threw him into the water and the waves quieted down.

Shining Star Publications. Copyright © 1994

SS3846

Jonah did not drown as they had expected. The Lord had provided a huge fish to swallow him. For three days and three nights Jonah was inside the fish, but he was not hurt. He prayed and thanked God for saving him. Then God commanded the great fish to spit Jonah up onto dry land.

As soon as Jonah was on dry ground, the Lord gave him a second chance to do what he was supposed to. This time Jonah did what God told him; he went to Nineveh. For three days he walked around the city, warning everybody to turn from their evil ways.

After hearing Jonah, everybody, even the king, believed the warning. The people took off their expensive robes and put on mourning clothes. They fasted and prayed.

When God saw that they had turned from their sin, He was pleased with them. He did not destroy their city as He had threatened. Because Jonah obeyed God, he saved a great city from destruction.

SS3846

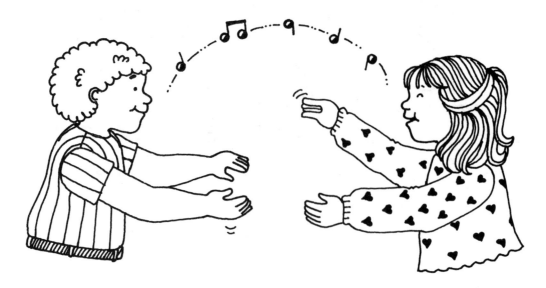

JONAH LEARNS TO LISTEN

Sing this song to the tune of "Twinkle, Twinkle, Little Star" while doing the motions.

Jonah heard what God did say,	*Cup hand around ear.*
But he tried to run away.	*Shake head.*
He did not listen to his Lord.	*Continue shaking head.*
Sailors threw him overboard.	*Pretend to throw something heavy with both hands.*
A great fish swallowed him down then	*Snap hands together like a large mouth closing.*
And brought him to the land again.	*Spread hands in welcoming gesture.*
Then Jonah did what God had said,	*Nod head.*
And Nineveh was saved instead.	*Clasp hands over head in victory gesture.*
Jonah learned to listen well	*Put hand to ear again.*
And do whatever God should tell.	*Shake finger as if scolding.*

THE STORM AT SEA

Divide children into two lines. Give the first child in each line a doll representing Jonah. (This may be a clothespin doll or a paper doll.) Holding it in both hands, the first child passes it over his head (as if Jonah is on a high wave) to the next child's two hands. The second child passes the doll between his legs (as if Jonah is in the low trough between waves) to the third person. Continue over and under until the last child gets the doll, runs to the front, and starts "Jonah" back again. The "storm" ends when one line gets all its players back into their original places. The whole class may share the prize of a package of "gummy fish" or fish-shaped crackers.

CALMING THE STORM
Based on Mark 4:35-41

One time Jesus had been busy all day talking with people and teaching them. When evening came, He was very tired. He said to His disciples, "Let's go over to the other side of the lake where it's quiet."

The disciples thought that was a good idea. They always liked to be alone with Jesus. They all walked down to the edge of the Sea of Galilee, where there were fishing boats. Jesus got into one boat with a few of His followers. The others got into other boats, and they all started across the water.

Jesus was so tired that He took a cushion to the stern of the boat, lay down, and went to sleep. The disciples set the sails and started across the lake.

By the time they were halfway across the Sea of Galilee, the wind began to blow hard. It blew harder and harder. The waves rolled up higher and higher. The disciples took the sails down. Still the wind kept tipping the boat. Water dashed over its sides, and it was almost swamped. The disciples tried to bail it out, but more waves came splashing in. Jesus slept right through the storm.

His disciples didn't want to disturb Him, but they were afraid the boat was going to sink. They came to the back of the boat where Jesus was sleeping and woke Him up. "Teacher," they said, "don't you care if we drown?"

Before He answered them, Jesus stood up and spoke to the waves. "Be still!" He said. The wind quieted down, and so did the waves.

SS3846

The disciples were amazed to see the waves become calm and the sea become quiet at His words.

Then Jesus turned to His disciples and asked, "Why are you so afraid? Do you still not have faith?"

They didn't know how to answer Him. They were awed by His power to quiet the storm. His power was greater than the power of the wind and the waves! His followers had seen other wonderful things Jesus had done. Still, they had not had any idea how very great His power really was. They hardly felt they knew Him. They looked at one another and asked, "Who is this? Even the wind and the waves obey Him!"

Jesus still calms people's fears. If we turn to Him when we are in trouble, He can help us feel quiet just as He did the wind and the waves on the Sea of Galilee.

SOUND ASLEEP

Use the motions as you sing this song to the tune of "Here We Go 'Round the Mulberry Bush."

Jesus was sound asleep one night,
Asleep one night, asleep one night.
Jesus was sound asleep one night
On the Sea of Galilee.

Lean face, with eyes shut, on folded hands.

A terrible storm came up that night,
Came up that night, came up that night.
A terrible storm came up that night
On the Sea of Galilee.

Swing arms back and forth wildly.

When Jesus awoke, He calmed the storm,
He calmed the storm, He calmed the storm.
When Jesus awoke, He calmed the storm
On the Sea of Galilee.

Move hands, palms down, gently back and forth.

So Jesus will calm our terrible fears,
Our terrible fears, our terrible fears.
So Jesus will calm our terrible fears,
Like the Sea of Galilee.

Lean face, with eyes open, on folded hands.

CALMING THE WAVES

Set a big tub in the middle of the room to represent the disciples' boat. Have all the children stand in a circle around it (not too near), each holding a ball with his or her name taped on it. (These may be rubber balls, tennis balls, or basketballs, depending on availability and the manual dexterity of the children.) Each child tries to bounce the ball once and make it go into the boat. (This is harder than throwing directly into the tub, but gives more of the effect of waves bouncing into the boat.) Whoever misses, recaptures the ball and tries again, making more waves. The game goes on until the teacher calls, "Peace, be still." Then everyone stops and winners are announced as the balls are taken from the tub.

SS3846

JESUS IN THE TEMPLE
Based on Luke 2:41-52

Every spring Mary and Joseph went to Jerusalem for the celebration of the Passover (a special festival held in memory of the Israelites' escape from slavery in Egypt). When He was old enough, they took Jesus with them. Lots of their friends and relatives were going too. Some people walked and some rode donkeys, but they all had a good time on the way. They talked and told stories and sang psalms.

Mary and Joseph were in Jerusalem two or three days. After the celebration was over, they started back to Nazareth. On the way home, Mary and Joseph realized that Jesus was not with them, but they thought He was with some of His cousins in the crowd.

That evening though, when He did not arrive for supper, Mary and Joseph were worried. They went through the crowd, asking all their friends and relatives if Jesus was with them. Nobody had seen Him.

The next morning when everybody else went on towards Nazareth, Mary and Joseph left the crowd. They went back to Jerusalem to try to find Jesus. They spent three days looking and asking people along the way and in the city. They were getting very worried and upset.

At last they found Him, sitting in one of the temple courtyards, asking the teachers questions and talking with them. People who heard Him said afterwards that they were amazed at this boy's questions and answers.

SS3846

As soon as she could get to Him, Mary said to Jesus, "My son, why have You treated us like this? You knew it was time to be going home. Your father and I have been worried. We have been looking everywhere for You."

Jesus just asked them a question: "Why have you been searching for me? Didn't you know I would be here in my Father's house?"

Mary and Joseph did not really understand what He meant, but Mary kept thinking about what He had said.

Jesus went with Mary and Joseph back to Nazareth. He was twelve years old and beginning to grow up. The Bible says He "grew in wisdom and in stature" — that means His mind was growing and learning to think more, and His body was growing taller and stronger. The Bible also says He grew "in favor with God and man." That means He did what God wanted Him to do, and everybody liked Him. Jesus was growing in every way.

HE GREW IN WISDOM AND STATURE

What the Bible says about how Jesus grew should be true for all of us who are still growing. Let's all say it together to help us remember it. (Ask for a volunteer to read the solo lines. Have the rest of the group speak the chorus lines.)

Solo: When Jesus was just a little boy,

Chorus: He grew in wisdom and stature
And in favor with God and man.

Solo: When Jesus was a bigger boy,

Chorus: He grew in wisdom and stature
And in favor with God and man.

Solo: Now Jesus wants every one of us blest

Chorus: As we grow in wisdom and stature
And in favor with God and man.

Solo: So we promise that we will do our best

Chorus: To grow in wisdom and stature
And in favor with God and man.

JESUS IS MISSING

Mary or Joseph is trying to find Jesus to take Him home. Seat half of the group in a circle of chairs, leaving one chair empty. The rest of the group stand, one behind each chair, including the empty one left for their son. All those standing must have their hands clasped behind them.

Whoever stands behind the empty chair tries to get his "son" to sit there. He looks around the circle and suddenly says to one of the seated persons, "Come." That one tries to run to the empty chair, but the one back of him grabs for his shoulders and tries to hold him in the chair. If he succeeds, "Joseph" or "Mary" tries someone else. If he loses the seated person, he becomes Joseph or Mary and tries to bring someone else to the empty chair.

THE GREAT CATCH OF FISH
Based on Luke 5:1-11

Sometimes Jesus taught people in the synagogues of the villages where He went. Other times He talked to people out in the countryside. After He became well-known, He had to teach outdoors because the crowds of people who wanted to hear Him were too big to get in a building.

One day Jesus was standing by the Sea of Galilee talking to people. Everybody wanted to get close to Him. Some wanted to hear what He was saying; others wanted to be healed. The trouble was, the more they crowded close to Him, the harder it was for Him to make all of them hear.

Then He noticed two boats nearby at the edge of the water. Their owners were not in them. They were on the beach mending their fishnets. Jesus didn't think they would mind letting Him use a boat for a little while. He stepped into one of the boats and pushed it out into the water. Nobody else could get in, but everybody could see and hear Him.

When He had finished talking, Jesus wanted to do something for Simon to thank him for the use of his boat. (Simon, who was also called Peter, was one of the fishermen mending his nets.) Jesus said to him, "Pull out into deeper water and let down your nets for a load of fish."

Simon Peter shook his head and said, "Master, we have worked all night and haven't caught any." Then he changed his mind. He said, "Still, if You say so, I'll try again."

He and his helpers rowed the boat out a little ways. Then they threw out the nets. They caught so many fish the nets began to break. Simon called to the other fishermen, "Bring the second boat!" His friends brought the boat as fast as they could, and helped pull the nets in. The two boats were filled so full they were almost ready to sink!

Simon Peter bowed down to Jesus and told Him to go away. He said Jesus was too wonderful to be with a sinner such as he.

Jesus told him, "Don't worry. From now on you will not catch just fish, you will fish for men."

Simon Peter and his friends pulled their boats in to shore where they left them to follow Jesus. From then on they were fishers of men, just as Jesus had told them. They were the first disciples.

They told many people about Jesus. Their stories of Jesus caught people's attention just the way they had caught fish before. They "caught" people for Jesus.

CATCHING THE FISH

Choose one child to be a fish; all the others are fishermen. The fish carries a package of fish-shaped crackers. The fishermen join hands in a long line. Their objective is to get the first and last fisherman to join hands, making a circular "net" with the fish inside the circle. The fish tries to avoid being surrounded. When he is finally encircled, he shares the crackers with the ones who caught him.

FISHERS OF MEN

With motions, sing this song to the tune of "This Old Man."

Fishermen	
Cast their net,	*Broad arm motion.*
But the fish they could not get.	*Shake head.*
Hauled hard, threw their nets —	*Pulling, then throwing motions.*
Anywhere would do.	*Shrug.*
Caught no fish	*Shake head and move hands in front*
The whole night through.	*of body, palms down.*
Jesus called,	*Hand to side of mouth.*
"Come to Me.	*Beckon.*
Leave your boats there by the sea.	*Point with right arm.*
Pray and show your faith	*Point to mouth.*
Anyway you wish.	*Hands, palm up, in front; shrug.*
You will catch	*Arms in wide inclusive gesture.*
More men than fish."	

JESUS HEALS THE PARALYZED MAN

Based on Luke 5:17-26

One day Jesus was teaching in a house in Capernaum. People had come from all over Galilee and Judea to hear Him. Lawyers and Pharisees were listening. (Pharisees were Jewish religious leaders.) Such a crowd had gathered that nobody else could get near Jesus.

Some men were late getting there. They had brought a paralyzed friend to have Jesus heal him. He could not move or stand up. They were late because they had carried their friend all the way on his bed. (The beds in those days were like pads or gym mats.) Each of the friends had carried one corner of the mat with the sick man lying on it.

When they got to the house, so many people were crowded around, they could not get in. What could they do? They had carried their friend all the way from his house. They were sure Jesus would heal him if they could just get near.

Then one of the men had an idea. "Let's take some of the tiles off the roof," he said. "We can put them back afterwards. If we let the bed down through the roof, everybody will have to move to make room for it."

The others agreed. They went around to the side where the stairs led up to the flat roof. Quickly they pried up the tiles. Then carefully they lowered the bed with their friend on it right down in front of Jesus.

Everybody else was surprised, but Jesus was pleased. He realized that they had faith enough to work hard in order to get their friend to Him. He looked down at the sick man on the mat and said, "Friend, your sins are forgiven."

Nobody had expected Him to say that. The Pharisees and the lawyers thought Jesus had no right to say it. They were thinking that only God could forgive sins.

Jesus knew what they were thinking. He wanted them to learn something they had not thought about. Because He was the Son of God, Jesus could forgive sins. He asked the people around Him, "Which is easier, to say 'Your sins are forgiven,' or 'Get up and walk'?"

Nobody answered Him. He looked down at the paralyzed man again and said, "I tell you, get up. Take up your mat and go home."

At once the sick man was able to stand. He picked up the mat he had been lying on. Then he praised God for his healing. He looked around for his friends; then he went home to his family. Everybody else was praising God, too, for the wonderful healing they had seen that day.

A SICK MAN'S FRIENDS

Have the children sing this song to the tune of "Hush, Little Baby."

A sick man's friends said, "We know how you feel.
We'll take you to Jesus, for He can heal.

"If you can't walk, we'll carry you instead.
We'll take you there on your very own bed.

"If we can't get to Him on the ground,
We'll take you to the rooftop and let you down.

"And He will heal and forgive your sin,
So you can stand up and walk again."

And that's what they did; Jesus healed the man.
He stood and thanked God; then home he ran.

CARRYING A SICK MAN

To help class members see what a difficult task the friends of the sick man undertook, try this race.

Divide children into groups of four. Give each group a newspaper page to represent the bed. Each child takes one corner. On the bed place a crumpled piece of tissue paper to represent the man. (This light weight will blow off if they move too fast.) At the signal, each group of four starts across the room. They must keep their "bed" flat enough and move slowly enough that they do not spill the man from his bed, nor hold the corners so far up that he is uncomfortable in the middle. The first group that gets across the room wins, of course. If some stairs are safely available, the four may be required to go up a few steps and let their friend down carefully, before their task is done.

THE CENTURION'S FAITH

Based on Luke 7:1-10

Jesus often went to Capernaum, a city near the Sea of Galilee. The Jewish people there knew Him well. They called Him "Rabbi," which meant "Teacher." Even the Roman officials who governed the city had heard of Jesus.

Once the servant of a Roman centurion was very sick. (A centurion was an army officer.) The centurion was afraid his servant might die. He really cared about his servant, but no doctor had been able to help him.

Then somebody told the centurion that Jesus had just returned to Capernaum. The Roman centurion had heard about the healing Jesus had done. He was sure Jesus could cure his servant.

Still, he didn't want to go ask Jesus himself. He thought a well-known rabbi like Jesus would not want to speak to a Roman. He knew that many Jewish people hated the Romans who ruled their country. He decided to ask some Jewish friends to ask Jesus to cure his servant.

His friends went to Jesus and told Him about the centurion's servant. They told Him what a good man the centurion was. They said he had even paid for the building of their synagogue. Jesus didn't hesitate when He was asked for help. He started for the centurion's house with the men who had talked to Him.

When the centurion saw Jesus coming, he sent another friend to tell Jesus not to bother to come all the way. The centurion believed that Jesus didn't need to touch the servant to heal him. All He had to do was to order the sickness to leave.

The centurion told his friend to say, "I know what orders mean. I have taken orders, and I give orders. When I tell a soldier, 'Go,' he goes; or, 'Come,' and he comes. I say to my servant, 'Do this' and he does it."

The messenger hurried to meet Jesus to tell Him what the Roman official had said. When Jesus heard him, He stood there amazed. He said to the men near Him, "I tell you, I have not found such great faith even in Israel."

Because the centurion had such great faith, Jesus didn't even have to go the rest of the way to his house. The servant was cured from that very minute.

THE POWER OF JESUS

Talk with the class about the people involved in this story and the different attitudes they had: the sick man, the centurion, the messengers, the people surrounding Jesus, etc. Let children volunteer for the various roles to do an impromptu dramatization of the incident.

THE CENTURION'S FAITH

Sing this song with the appropriate gestures to the tune of "The Muffin Man."

If I say, "Go," my soldiers go,	*Hold out right hand with finger*
My soldiers go, my soldiers go.	*pointing; then alternate with left at*
If I say, "Go," my soldiers go,	*each phrase.*
They do as I command.	*Salute.*
If You say, "Live," my servant lives,	*Hold out right arm with palm up;*
My servant lives, my servant lives.	*then alternate with left at each*
If You say, "Live," my servant lives.	*phrase.*
All life is in Your hands.	*Cup two hands in front and lift in*
	offering gesture.

JESUS HEALS A BLIND MAN
Based on Luke 18:35-43

Jesus often liked to teach outdoors. He didn't always teach inside a house or synagogue. One day He was walking toward Jericho with a lot of other people and talking with them. As they walked, they came near a blind man sitting beside the road and begging. He had no home to go to, and he couldn't see to work. All he could do was sit there and hope somebody would give him money or food.

There was such a crowd of people around Jesus that the blind man couldn't help hearing them talk, but he could not see who it was. "What is going on?" he called out.

Somebody told him, "Jesus of Nazareth is going by."

The blind man had heard of Jesus. He knew that sometimes Jesus healed people. He thought, "This is my chance!" He shouted, "Jesus, have mercy on me."

The people around Jesus thought the blind man wasn't very polite to yell at Him like that. They thought he shouldn't bother Jesus. They told the blind man to keep still.

He didn't pay any attention to them. He jumped up and shouted again, even louder, "Jesus, son of David, have mercy on me!" He couldn't see, so he couldn't tell which man was Jesus. If the blind man could have seen, he would have run to Jesus, knelt down, and asked more humbly for help. Instead, he just stood there and shouted.

This time Jesus heard him. He didn't know what the blind man wanted, but He was always ready to help people. He stopped right there in the road and said to one of His friends, "Bring the man who is shouting to Me." The friend went over to the side of the road where the blind man was standing. He took the man's arm and led him to Jesus.

Jesus said to him, "Why are you asking for mercy? What do you want Me to do for you?"

The blind man replied, "Lord, I want to see! I ask You to have mercy on me and heal my eyes so I can see."

Jesus said to him, "You shall see. Because you have faith that I can help you, you are healed."

Suddenly the man's eyes were healed, and he could see! He thanked God and praised Him as he followed Jesus. The man didn't have to sit by the side of the road and beg any more. Jesus had healed his blindness. Now he could see to work and to walk freely with people and to enjoy the beautiful world around him.

SS3846

WHAT DO YOU WANT TO SEE?

Ask children to shut their eyes, keep their hands over them for a minute, and think what the blind man would be most glad to see when he was healed. After opening their eyes, they can make a class list. A large class may be divided into groups who may compare their completed lists.

SEEING

Ask children to pretend they have been blind and have just regained their sight. Sing this song to the tune of "Three Blind Mice." It may be sung in unison or as a round.

Oh, my Lord, I can see
All the things You made for me.
I see the sun and the birds that fly.
I see the trees reaching branches high.
I see the moon in the starry sky.
And I thank You.
I thank You.

HAVE MERCY

Let children improvise a skit dramatizing this story. Have one child volunteer to sit on the floor, blindfolded. Have him keep asking for mercy or help while the other children try to keep him still. Another child may represent Jesus, asking what the blindfolded one wants. When the blindfolded one answers, the child representing Jesus takes off the other's blindfold and announces his healing. This may be done several times with different volunteers so that more than one will have the experience of regaining his sight.

ZACCHAEUS

Based on Luke 19:1-10

When Jesus was going through the city of Jericho, a crowd of people walked with Him, ahead of Him, behind Him, and on each side of Him. They made it hard for anybody else to get near, because they all wanted to see and hear Him.

One man especially wanted to see Jesus. His name was Zacchaeus. The trouble was that Zacchaeus was not a tall man. In fact, he was so short he could not see over the heads of the other people.

"I know what I'll do," he said to himself. He ran ahead to a sycamore tree which stood by the side of the road. He climbed up into the branches so he could easily see Jesus over the heads of the crowd.

He had not thought, though, that Jesus would be able to see him too. When the crowd came along by the tree, Jesus looked up and smiled at him. "Come down, Zacchaeus," He said. "I must stay at your house today."

Zacchaeus was so excited, he almost fell off the branch he was sitting on. He was in such a hurry to get down, he didn't care whether anybody else noticed him or not. He began welcoming Jesus to his house as soon as his feet touched the ground.

The people around Jesus were disgusted. They knew Zacchaeus was a tax collector and very rich. Many people hated tax collectors because they often cheated taxpayers. Everybody began to grumble. Why should Jesus go to the house of a tax collector? Why would He eat with a man they thought was a cheat and a sinner?

Zacchaeus knew what people thought about him, and he didn't want Jesus to be ashamed of him. He wanted to do what was right. He said, "My Lord, right now I promise to give half of my riches to help poor people. And if I have cheated anybody, I will give him back four times the amount — four times!"

Jesus was glad that Zacchaeus had repented and offered to help the people he had hurt. Jesus said to him, "Today salvation has come to this house. I have come to save what was lost."

Jesus wasn't talking about money that people had lost. He meant that Zacchaeus had been lost to God as long as he cheated people. Now that he believed in Jesus, he was willing to be honest and generous. Jesus could visit happily in his house. Jesus knew that Zacchaeus had cared enough to climb a tree to see Him and to do what was right.

OH, ZACCHAEUS

Sing this song to the tune of "Clementine," while doing the motions.

Oh, Zacchaeus, oh, Zacchaeus,
Was as short as he could be.   *Lean down, using right hand to*
When he wanted to see Jesus,   *measure distance from floor.*
He climbed up a sycamore tree.   *Raise left hand, fingers wiggling.*

Jesus saw him; Jesus called him,   *Beckon with right hand.*
"Come, Zacchaeus, come," said He.
And Zacchaeus, so delighted,
Jumped down from the sycamore tree.   *"Jump" left hand down.*

Then Zacchaeus, rich Zacchaeus,   *Clasp hands.*
Said to Jesus, "Please hear me.
I will give back lots of money."   *Spread out arms.*
Jesus said, "From sin be free."   *Raise right hand in blessing.*

Oh, Zacchaeus, oh, Zacchaeus,   *Nod head.*
He was glad as he could be   *Clasp hands.*
That he truly had seen Jesus   *Nod head.*
When he climbed the sycamore tree.   *Raise left hand, fingers wiggling.*

TAX TIME

Remind the class that many of the crowd who saw Zacchaeus with Jesus were people who had been cheated by tax collectors. They hated Zacchaeus because he was a tax collector and had perhaps cheated some of them.

Choose a child to be Zacchaeus. Divide the class, half on each side of the room behind a goal with Zacchaeus in the middle. When he calls, "Tax time," they all try to change sides without being tagged by him. The one caught must be the next Zacchaeus. The game may be brought to a close with the teacher, acting as Jesus, calling Zacchaeus to him and blessing him with a hand raised in a motion of forgiveness.

SS3846

FEEDING THE FIVE THOUSAND
Based on John 6:5-13

One day Jesus went across the Sea of Galilee with His disciples. He wanted them to rest and talk, but they had no chance.

Other people had seen where He was going. Most of the people didn't have boats, so they walked all the way around the lake to follow Him. Everybody was anxious to see what wonderful things Jesus might do. They wanted to hear His teaching.

When Jesus saw the crowd coming, He didn't send them away even though He was tired. He felt sorry for them. He saw that some were sick and others were very tired. They had come so far, and they would not be able to get home in time for supper. They would all be hungry.

Thinking about supper, Jesus asked one of His disciples where they could get bread for so many people. The disciple was shocked. He said they didn't have enough money, even if there had been a place to buy bread. "Why," he said, "if we had eight months' wages, we could not feed that crowd. There are too many!"

Another disciple, Andrew, spoke up. "There is one little boy here who has offered to share his supper," he said. "He has five small loaves his mother made from barley flour." (That would be like five little rolls or biscuits.) "Also," said Andrew, "he has two small fish. But what is that to feed so many? There must be five thousand men here, plus women and children!"

SS3846

Jesus smiled at him and said, "Bring the boy to me." Then He told His disciples to have everybody sit down on the grass in groups.

While everybody was finding a place, Andrew came back with the little boy. Jesus thanked the boy for being willing to share his supper, then He lifted the bread and the fish up in His hands. He thanked God for the food and for the little boy's generosity.

Jesus divided the bread and the fish and gave it to His disciples. They went among all the groups and gave everybody some to eat. Everybody had supper together, and there was so much food, after everybody had eaten the disciples gathered twelve baskets of leftover pieces of fish and bread.

This was such a great miracle that everybody talked about it. Years later, all four writers of the Gospels told about it too. We read this wonderful story of the five loaves and two fish that fed five thousand people, and it reminds us that God can take care of our needs, no matter what they are.

 SS3846

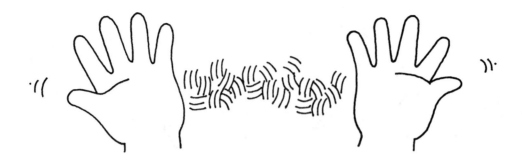

ONE LITTLE BOY

Leader: Everybody do as I do:

This is the one little boy who shared his supper.	*Hold up one finger.*
These are the two little fish in his basket.	*Hold up two fingers of other hand.*
These are the five little loaves of bread.	*Hold up five fingers of first hand.*
And these are the thousands and thousands and thousands and thousands and thousands of people . . .	*Open and shut all fingers of both hands for each "thousands." Do it faster and faster. Children's laughter will help them remember the huge number of people.*
. . . who all shared five loaves and two fish with one little boy.	*Hold up five fingers.* *Hold up two fingers.* *Hold up one finger.*

FIVE LOAVES AND TWO FISH

Sing to the tune of "John Brown's Body."

Five thousand people followed Jesus 'round the sea.
Five thousand people followed Jesus 'round the sea.
Five thousand people followed Jesus 'round the sea.
'Twas the Sea of Galiliee.

One small boy had brought a basket with some lunch.
(Repeat twice.)
But how could that feed this bunch?

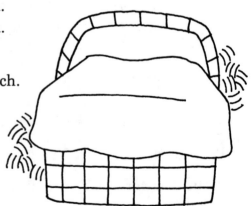

Five small loaves of bread and two tiny fish.
(Repeat twice.)
But to share them was his wish.

"Thank You, God," said Jesus as the people shared the food.
(Repeat twice.)
And they all ate and said it was good.

SS3846

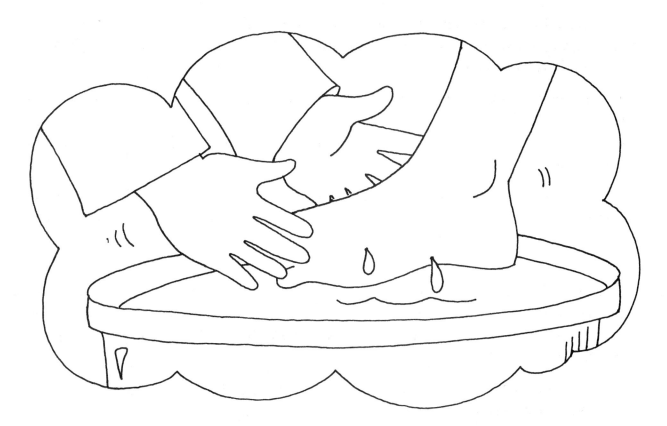

WASHING THE DISCIPLES' FEET

Based on John 13:3-17

In the days when Jesus lived in Palestine, most people walked barefoot or wore sandals. It was a warm country, so they didn't need socks and shoes. The trouble was that their feet got very hot and dusty. They needed to wash their feet when they went into anybody's house. Homeowners, to be polite, would give each guest a basin of water for washing the feet. If the person wanted to show special honor to someone, he would wash the guest's feet himself.

One evening Jesus was having supper with His disciples. Suddenly He thought of a way to teach them. He got up from the table and took off His outer robe. He tied a towel around His waist and brought a basin of water.

He washed the feet of several disciples and dried them with the towel. Peter was shocked at the idea of Jesus doing such a thing for him. He thought it should be the other way around, that he should serve Jesus.

Peter said, "Lord, are You really going to wash my feet?"

Jesus answered, "You don't realize now why I'm doing this. Later you will understand."

"Oh no," said Peter. "You shall never wash my feet!"

"Then you cannot be one of My followers," answered Jesus.

SS3846

That hurt Peter's feelings. He had wanted to be one of Jesus' followers from the day Jesus had first called him from his fishing. "If that is the way," he said, "wash my head and my hands as well."

Jesus said, "No, that is not needed." He didn't want them to think a bath was what He was talking about. He washed Peter's feet and those of the rest of the disciples. They were not sure why He was doing it, but they wanted to do whatever Jesus said they should.

When He had finished, He took the towel off His waist, put on His robe again, and sat down with them. Then He explained, "I have set you an example. You should follow it. If I am your Lord and Teacher, as you call Me, then you should do as I have done for you."

Of course, He didn't mean that they should wash everybody's feet. He meant that if He was willing to do little ordinary things to help other people, His followers should be too. He finished His teaching by saying, "Now that you know these things, you will be blessed if you do them."

Like the disciples, we need to learn what Jesus wants us to do, and we need to do things for other people as He did.

SS3846

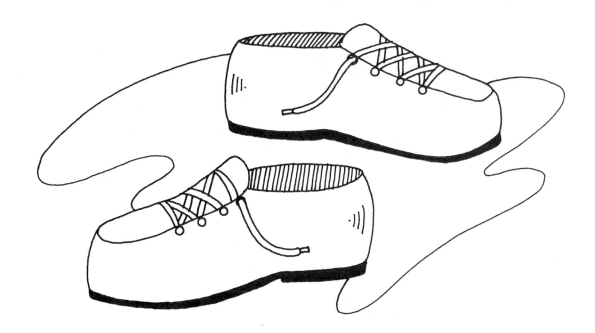

MY FEET

Help children read or recite this prayer; then repeat it with the motions.

Sometimes I march,   *March in place*
Or I tiptoe;   *Tiptoe in place.*
Sometimes I run   *Run in place.*
Wherever I go.

Please lead my feet   *Stand with hands folded as if in*
Where they should go   *prayer, but look down at feet as the*
As You did the disciples'   *group moves into a prayer circle.*
So long ago.

PETER SPEAKS

Using the motions, sing this song to the tune of "The Farmer in the Dell."

Jesus washed my feet.   *Have children stand in a row and point*
Jesus washed my feet.   *to their feet during the first two lines.*
I was His disciple   *Put hand on heart in gesture of allegiance.*
When Jesus washed my feet.   *Point to feet again.*

He showed, "To serve is sweet." *Hold out arms during first two lines.*
He showed, "To serve is sweet."
I am His disciple,   *Put hand on heart again.*
For Jesus washed my feet.   *Keep hand on heart while pointing to*
                                   feet again with other hand.

SS3846

FEED MY SHEEP

Based on John 21:4-17

Early one morning after Jesus was resurrected, He went to the Sea of Galilee. Some of His disciples were fishing from their boats. Jesus wanted to see Peter and the others. He had something special to tell them.

At first they did not realize that the man on the shore was Jesus. He called out to them, "Friends, do you have any fish?"

They said, "No, it has been a poor night for fishing."

"Throw out your nets on the right side of the boat," He called. While they were doing that, Jesus built a little fire. He was going to broil fish for their breakfast.

When they tried to pull their net in, it was so full of fish they couldn't get it into the boat. Then they realized that it was not a stranger there on shore — it was Jesus. He had helped them find all those fish.

Peter was so excited, he jumped right into the water and swam to shore as fast as he could. The other disciples brought the boat to shore, towing the net full of fish behind them.

Jesus told them to bring some fish to cook on the fire. He had some bread ready. Peter rushed back to the boat and helped pull the net full of fish to shore. He was so anxious to do what Jesus asked that he couldn't wait.

SS3846

The fish were soon cooked and some bread toasted over the fire. Jesus gave food to each of the men. They were so happy to see Him again, they couldn't seem to say anything. They didn't need to ask who He was or why He was doing this. They knew He was Jesus, and they were happy to be eating together with Him again.

Jesus spoke to Peter directly. "Do you love Me?" He asked.

Peter replied, "Of course I love You. You know I do."

Then Jesus told him how he could show that love. "Feed My lambs," He said. He meant for Peter to do for other people as Jesus was doing for him.

Some time before that, Jesus had told His followers that He was like a shepherd who always loves and takes care of his sheep. Now He wanted Peter and the others to remember. To make sure Peter understood, He asked again, "Do you love Me?"

Peter answered, "You know, Lord, that I love You."

Again Jesus said to Peter, "Feed My sheep." He wanted Peter to remember that just saying he loved Jesus was not enough. He must help take care of Jesus' followers.

Finally He asked Peter again — this was the third time — "Do you love Me?"

Peter was hurt that Jesus doubted him, but he answered again, "Truly, Lord, I love You."

For the third time Jesus told him, "Feed My sheep."

Peter never forgot that. We need to remember it too. If we love Jesus, we will help take care of His followers.

FEED MY LAMBS

Divide the group into pairs. Use the "Pease Porridge Hot" hand motions as you say the words Jesus said to Peter.

Feed	*Hands flat on lap.*
My	*Hands clap together.*
lambs.	*Hands clap teammate's hands.*
Feed	*Hands flat on lap.*
My	*Hands together.*
sheep.	*Hands clap teammate's hands.*
If	*Hands flat on lap.*
you	*Hands together.*
love	*Right hand claps teammate's right hand.*
Me,	*Own hands together.*
Feed	*Left hand claps teammate's left hand.*
My	*Own hands together.*
sheep.	*Both hands clap teammate's hands.*

FEED MY SHEEP

Sing these instructions of Jesus to the tune of "Three Blind Mice."

Feed My lambs.
Feed My sheep.
See what they need.
See what they need.

They all need food and good water too.
They need to have much loving care from you.
Look around and see all that you can do,
And feed My sheep!

PARABLE OF THE SOWER
Based on Matthew 13:3-9, 18-23

Jesus told a story about a man who went out to plant grain in his fields. Today we would have a big machine to plant the grain. In Bible times, a man just took a bag of seeds and threw them out, a handful at a time.

At first, the man let some seeds fall right on the path where he was walking. Birds could see them easily. They came fluttering down and ate up all the seeds. Those seeds never had a chance to grow.

Then the man went farther into the field and sowed grain there. That field had stony ground. The seeds sprouted and started to grow, but the soil was so thin over the stones, the sun burned the seeds' roots. They could not grow; they just wilted and died.

Next the man sowed some seeds in better ground. The seeds sprang up fast, but so did the weeds. In fact, the weeds grew faster. They grew so big that they overshadowed the stalks of grain and choked them out.

The man sowed his last seeds on the best ground where they grew and grew. When they were harvested, they amounted to bushels of grain. Some of the fields had thirty, some sixty, and some a hundred times as much grain as the man had sowed.

This story that Jesus told is about more than just planting seeds in the ground. It is called a parable because it teaches us a special lesson. The seeds in the story represent the words Jesus spoke. His words tell us how to do His will. When His disciples asked what the story meant, Jesus explained it to them this way.

SS3846

He told them that the birds that ate the seeds before they could grow were like Satan, snatching away the words of Jesus before people have time to think and understand them. The seeds on stony ground did a little better. They were like Jesus' words that someone gladly hears, but they do not "stick" and help that person make a life change. Like the seeds on stony ground, they have no deep roots.

The third bunch of seeds got choked out by all kinds of other things. They represent Jesus' words starting to grow well in a person's life, then they are forgotten because of worries. The worries are like weeds. Sometimes people forget the words of Jesus because of other exciting things that happen. Exciting things can be like weeds, crowding out the teachings of Jesus.

The last seeds were best of all. They grew in good ground. They are like the good things that happen when we remember to do what Jesus tells us. We grow as Christians, like the seeds, and do bushels and bushels of good!

THE SOWER

Sing this song to the tune of "My Bonnie Lies Over the Ocean" while doing the motions.

A man sowed a handful of grain seeds,   *Throw right arm out.*
But birds came and gobbled them down;   *Wiggle fingers as arm returns.*
Then he sowed more seeds, but they wilted.   *Throw right arm out.*
The sun scorched their roots dry and brown.   *Droop fingers.*
Sun scorched . . . sun scorched . . .   *Continue drooping fingers.*
The sun scorched their roots dry and brown.
Sun scorched . . . sun scorched . . .
The sun scorched their roots dry and brown.

He sowed still more seeds among thistles,   *Throw right arm out.*
The weeds choked the small grains of wheat.   *Droop fingers.*
Then he sowed his last seeds in some good ground;   *Throw right arm out.*
They made bushels of good grain to eat.   *Join hands in big circle.*
Good grain . . . good grain . . .   *Put hands to mouth and smile.*
They made bushels of good grain to eat.
Good grain . . . good grain . . .
They made bushels of good grain to eat.

I want to be good ground for Jesus.   *Point to self.*
I'll hear all the good words He sows.   *Cup hand to ear.*
I'll do bushels and bushels of good things,   *Join arms in big circle.*
And make sure that His good seeds all grow.   *Throw right arm out. Return*
All grow . . . all grow . . .   *arms with fingers open and up.*
And make sure that His good seeds all grow.
All grow . . . all grow . . .
And make sure that His good seeds all grow.

SOWING SEEDS

Draw five chalk lines on the floor at decreasing distances. Mark the nearest space (widest) 1 point; the second, 2 points; the third, 4; and the farthest (narrowest), 8. Give each child 10 seeds (peas or beans, not tiny seeds). Standing behind the tossing line, the child throws his seeds. His score depends on where his seeds land.

Shining Star Publications, Copyright © 1994

SS3846

PARABLE OF THE TALENTS
Based on Matthew 25:14-30

This is a story Jesus told His disciples. He wanted them to think about what they should do in this world.

One day a businessman decided to go on a trip. He wanted his business to keep making money while he was away, so he called in three of his workers and told them to take charge of his business for him.

To the most important worker, he gave five talents. (A talent was an amount of money.) To the next worker, the owner gave two talents. To the third worker, the businessman gave one talent.

Then he went on his journey and left these three men to look after his business. He was gone a long time.

While he was away, his worker who had five talents worked hard and made five more. The man who had two talents also worked hard, and he made two more. The man with only one talent was afraid he might lose that one, so he dug a hole in the ground and buried it.

At last the businessman came home. He called his workers to him and asked how they had managed his business.

The first worker said, "My lord, you gave me five talents, and I have used them to make five more. Here are ten talents."

The businessman said, "You have done well. You are a good and faithful servant."

Then the second worker said, "My lord, you gave me two talents, and I have made two more. Here are four talents."

The businessman said, "You also have done well. You are a good and faithful servant."

Then the third worker brought the one talent he had been given. "My lord," he said, "here is the talent you gave me. I was afraid it might be lost or stolen, so I hid it in the ground. I didn't use it at all."

The owner of the business was angry. He said, "You are a lazy and faithless servant, not to use the talent I gave you."

He turned to the people who were listening and said, "Take his one talent away and give it to the man who has ten. Everyone who uses his talents will be given more. He will work happily with me. But a man who doesn't use even one talent will have that one taken away."

Today the word *talent* means an ability. Maybe you have a talent for swimming or cooking or singing. The first two men in Jesus' parable used their abilities, so they learned to do even more in their business. But the man who didn't use his ability — his talent — forgot even how to do that one thing. Can you think what talents you have? How do you use them?

HOW MANY TALENTS?

Before telling the story, ask children to make the following motions during the story:

1. Each time a number of talents is mentioned, hold up the appropriate number of fingers.

2. Applaud after each "good and faithful servant."

3. At the condemnation of the third servant, point thumbs down.

TALENTED PEOPLE

After telling the story, help the class make a list of people they think have used their talents for the Lord (family, friends, sports figures, etc.). Include in the list the number and kinds of talents each one has used.

USE YOUR TALENTS

Sing this song with the motions to the tune of "Sweetly Sings the Donkey."

If you have five talents,
Hold up five fingers.
Use them every day.
Nod head.
If you do, you'll have fun,
Pull lips into a smile.
And the Lord will say,
"Well done, well done,
Pat hand on head in blessing at each
Well done, well done, well done!"
repetition.

If you have two talents,
Hold up two fingers.
Use them every day.
Nod.
If you do, you'll have fun,
Pull lips into smile.
And the Lord will say,
"Well done, well done,
Pat hand on head in blessing at each
Well done, well done, well done."
repetition.

If you have one talent,
Hold up one finger.
Use it every day.
Nod.
If you do, you'll have fun,
Pull lips into smile.
And the Lord will say,
"Well done, well done,
Pat hand on head in blessing at each
Well done, well done, well done."
repetition.

PARABLE OF THE GOOD SAMARITAN
Based on Luke 10:25-37

A man once said to Jesus, "The Bible tells us to love God and to love our neighbors. Who is my neighbor?"

Jesus wanted that man — and all the rest of us — to understand what it meant to be good neighbors. So, instead of answering the man's question, Jesus told him a story.

A Jewish man was going from Jerusalem to Jericho when robbers attacked him. They took all his money and beat him so badly, he could not even walk. They left him right there in the road.

After a while a priest came along the road. Did he help the poor beaten man? No, he just walked around the man to the other side of the road and went on. He never touched the man lying in the road. Maybe he didn't want to get dirty.

A little while later a Levite came along the road. (A Levite was an assistant to the priests, a special worker in the temple.) You would think he would help the poor injured man, wouldn't you? No, he didn't want to be bothered. He, too, just walked around to the other side of the road and went on his way.

Finally, a Samaritan came along. Many Jewish people didn't like Samaritans. They thought Samaritans didn't worship God properly and didn't follow all the Jewish laws.

The Samaritan certainly wouldn't help, would he? But he did! When he saw the poor man lying in the road, he got down off his donkey and went over to him. He took a bottle of oil and a bottle of wine out of his saddlebags. He used them like medicine, pouring them on the man's cuts where he was bleeding. Then he bandaged the man's wounds and lifted him up onto his own donkey. This good Samaritan walked the rest of the way to an inn, a place the injured man could stay for the night. He led the donkey, holding the man on the donkey's back.

The next morning the Samaritan had to go on about his business. The man who had been beaten wasn't able to go yet. The good Samaritan gave the innkeeper two silver coins. "Look after this poor man," he said, "and if it costs you any more, I will pay when I come again."

When Jesus had finished this story, he asked, "Which of these three men — the priest, the Levite, or the Samaritan — was a neighbor to the man who had been attacked?"

The man who had asked the question in the first place answered, "The one who was kind to him."

Jesus agreed and told him to go and do the same. That's what we all should do if we are going to be good neighbors.

GOOD NEIGHBORS

Start a discussion about people who have been "Good Samaritans" to your pupils. Pupils may be eager to give examples, but if they are slow to respond, prime them with some questions. Who is a good neighbor when you cross the street? Was somebody a good neighbor when you went to the dentist's office? Can a nurse be a good neighbor? A policeman? Does a good neighbor have to live right next to you?

SAMARITAN

Form a circle with all the children except one. Blindfold that one and put him in the center of the circle. As he calls out, "Jericho," the whole group circles to the right. After a few seconds, he calls, "Robber!" The circle stops at once, and the center person points and calls, "Neighbor!"

Whomever he is pointing at must tell how someone has been a neighbor to him. If he can't think of anybody, then he becomes the blindfolded one, and the game goes on. If he does tell of someone's help, he is given a construction paper crown with a big S on it. The game continues until all have "Samaritan" crowns, or time runs out.

HELP!

Have children sing this song to the tune of "Row, Row, Row Your Boat," in unison or as a round. If you want to use motions, have everybody join hands in a circle around one child lying on the floor. At the last line of the song, they all kneel and reach out their hands to the "injured" one.

Help! Help! Help the man
Lying in the dust.
To be a good Samaritan,
Help him now we must.

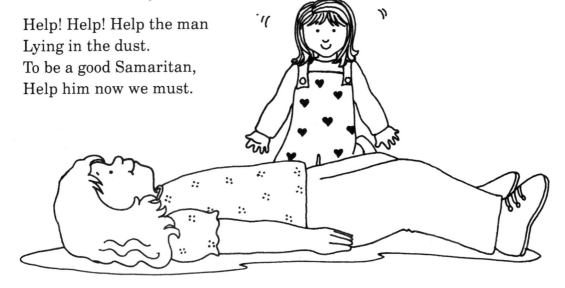

PARABLE OF THE LOST SHEEP

Based on Luke 15:3-7

The Pharisees were men who tried to be good and do everything right. They tried to follow every rule. They didn't want anything to do with people who broke the rules.

One day some Pharisees were complaining about Jesus. They said He welcomed sinners and talked with them. Sometimes He even ate dinner with them!

Jesus knew what they said about Him and about the people He ate dinner with. He didn't care about Himself, but He did care about the other people. He cared about the Pharisees too. Jesus knew they tried to do all the things they should. But He wanted them to understand something more. He knew that just following the rules wasn't enough. It was more important to love people and take care of them. Jesus told them a story to explain why He talked and ate with people who didn't always do right.

He said, "Suppose one of you had a hundred sheep. If you were a good shepherd, you would know every one of your sheep by name. You would take care of all of them. Now, suppose one of your sheep got lost, and you could not find it. You would miss that one, even though you still had ninety-nine others.

"You would look everywhere for the lost one. You would be afraid it had been caught in the briars or had fallen into a pit or a wolf had caught it or something else bad had happened to it.

"You would hunt and hunt for that lost sheep. When you found it, no matter where it was or what had happened — even if its wool were all dirty or full of thorns — you would pick it up, put it on your shoulders, and carry it home. Even if it made your robe dirty, you wouldn't care. You would just be glad you had found your sheep!

"You would be so glad, you would call in all the neighbors. 'Come, friends,' you would say, 'let us rejoice. Let's have a party to celebrate finding my lost sheep.'"

Then Jesus told His listeners, "That's the way it will be in heaven. There will be much happiness if a single sinner repents and is brought home like the sheep, even though there are ninety-nine already there. That is why I talk with people and eat with people who are lost. I am their shepherd, and I want to bring My lost sheep home to God."

SS3846

A HUNDRED SHEEP

Sing this song to the tune of "Mary Had a Little Lamb" while doing the motions.

A man who had a hundred sheep,
Hundred sheep, hundred sheep;
A man who had a hundred sheep
Lost one of them one day.

Extend arms in wide, inclusive motion.

Hold up one finger.

He hunted for his poor lost sheep,
Poor lost sheep, poor lost sheep;
He hunted for his poor lost sheep,
That had wandered far away.

*Shade eyes with hand at forehead
while looking from side to side.*

At last he found his one lost sheep,
One lost sheep, one lost sheep;
At last he found his one lost sheep
On cold and stony ground.

Hold up one finger.

He picked it up and took it home,
Took it home, took it home;
He picked it up and took it home,
So glad his sheep was found!

*Cross arms in carrying or hugging
position.*

LOST SHEEP GAME

String a small toy lamb on a long cord. Tie the ends of the cord together to make a big circle. Choose a child to be the shepherd. He stands blindfolded in the center of the circle while all other players take hold of the string and move their hands back and forth along it. One is holding the lamb hidden and passes it to his neighbor's hand.

When all are ready, the shepherd calls out, "Where is my little lost lamb?" and takes off the blindfold. He tries to see where the lamb is. All hands are moving back and forth to distract him as the lamb is passed secretly along the string. When the shepherd points at a person, that one must open his hands. If he has the sheep, he becomes the shepherd, and the former shepherd joins the circle. If not, the shepherd tries again.

PARABLE OF THE LOST SON

Based on Luke 15:11-24

Jesus often told stories, or parables, to make people realize how important they are to God and how much God loves them. This story is about a young man whose father thought he was lost.

A young man was bored with staying home and doing what his father told him. He wanted some excitement. He didn't want to wait until his father died in order to inherit his money. One day he said to his father, "Why don't you divide your property and give me my share now?"

Of course, this question hurt his father's feelings. But the father loved his son and wanted him to be happy. He divided his property and gave his son his share of it.

The young man took all his money and set off to find some excitement. He traveled to a distant country and spent all he had having a wild time.

Suddenly his money was all gone. What could the young man do? He didn't even have enough to buy food.

He was able to get a job, though it wasn't a very good one. He had to go out in the field and feed the pigs! He was so hungry, he wished he could have some of the pig food! But the pigs gobbled it all up, and nobody gave him anything.

The young man began to think. He knew that his father's workers were always given plenty of food. He made up his mind to go home. He was ashamed of the way he had wasted his money. He thought, "I will tell my father I have sinned against him and

against heaven. I don't even expect to be called his son anymore. I'll ask him to hire me as one of his workers."

The young man left his job feeding pigs and started toward home. It took him quite a while to get there, but as soon as he came in sight of the house, his father rushed out to him. He hugged his son and kissed him. He was so glad to see him again!

The young man tried to apologize and ask for a job as he had planned. His father didn't listen. He called to a servant and told him to bring a good robe and new sandals for his son. He put a ring on his son's finger. He called another servant and told him to kill a calf and start roasting it for a feast.

The father said, "My son was dead to me, but he has come alive. He was lost, but now he's found."

"That," said Jesus, "is the way God feels when you are sorry about the bad things you have done. He welcomes you when you come back to Him, as the father welcomed back his long lost son."

SS3846

THE LOST SON

After the story has been told once, explain pantomime — action that shows a story without actors speaking — to the children. Ask for two volunteers to be the father and his son. Reread or retell the story with these two acting it out. It may be done several times with different participants.

"HOW SOON CAN THE LOST SON GET HOME?" GAME

Remind children that the young man had no money and probably had a long, hard walk to get home. Give each child two pieces of paper about 8½" x 11" (newsprint or scrap typing paper) to represent the sand and stones he would have to walk on. Line up children across one end of the room. "Home" will be the opposite end.

As the game starts, each child puts down a piece of paper and steps on it. Then he puts down the second piece of paper and steps on that. He picks up the first paper, puts it ahead of him and steps on it. He continues alternating and stepping on papers, until he gets home.

For a more mature group, complications may be placed along the route: going through another country (another room), going around a forest or a walled city (piled-up chairs or boxes), etc.

The first child to reach "home" is welcomed by the teacher (father) with a ring (gold cord) and a new robe (piece of fabric, drape, bathrobe). The welcome may even include sandals made of construction paper soles with twine to tie around the feet and ankles.

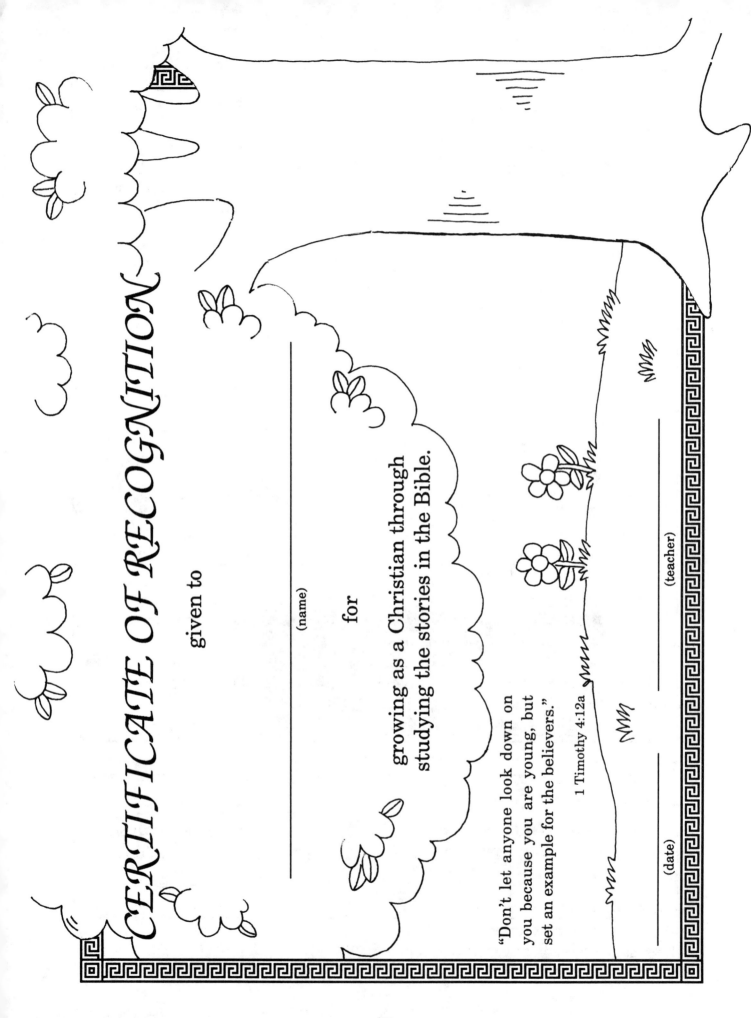

CERTIFICATE OF RECOGNITION

given to

_____
(name)

for

growing as a Christian through
studying the stories in the Bible.

"Don't let anyone look down on
you because you are young, but
set an example for the believers."
1 Timothy 4:12a

_____
(teacher)

_____
(date)

SS3846

Why did God give us so many good stories in the Bible?

"... that you may believe that Jesus is the Christ, the Son of God, and that by believing you may have life in his name." John 20:31

The stories in the Bible teach me to do what's right. I love to read it every day — morning, noon, and night.

Lord, teach me how to be what You want me to be.

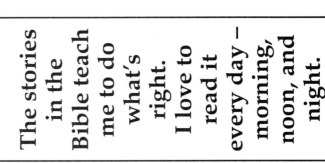

The more I study the Bible, the more I grow as a Christian.

Holy Bible

God's Word makes a difference in my life!

2 Timothy 3:16

SS3846